MOSSY OAK TRAIL GUIDE

MOSSY OAK TRAIL GUIDE

BARRY SNEED, GENERAL EDITOR

NAVPRESS

Discipleship Inside Out®

NAVPRESS ⊘

Discipleship Inside Out®

NavPress is the publishing ministry of The Navigators, an international Christian organization and leader in personal spiritual development. NavPress is committed to helping people grow spiritually and enjoy lives of meaning and hope through personal and group resources that are biblically rooted, culturally relevant, and highly practical.

For a free catalog go to www.NavPress.com
or call 1.800.366.7788 in the United States or 1.800.839.4769 in Canada.

ISBN-13: 978-1-61291-350-6
ISBN-13: 978-1-61291-455-8

Published in association with the literary agency of Alive Communications, Inc., 7680 Goddard St., Suite 200, Colorado Springs, CO 80920.

Printed in China

gift 09/2016

2 3 4 5 6 7 8 / 17 16 15 14 13

CONTENTS

A FEW HELPFUL HINTS ABOUT THIS GUIDE

This trail guide has been developed for you by NavPress in cooperation with Mossy Oak and ELEVÁRE International. Our hope is to be an inspiration to you as you read and share this practical guide for your life and outdoor activities.

This project exists in order to be a source of encouragement to all who come into contact with us. That encouragement comes as we create opportunities to serve others, love others, and give to others. We do this by investing in the lives of people and striving to make it obvious that the hope offered through this resource can change their lives.

Ecclesiastes 11:1 reminds us to "cast your bread upon the waters, for after many days you will find it again" (NIV).

This trail guide is an effort for us to do just that. We hope that you will find the information helpful — from scoring a Boone and Crockett whitetail deer to surviving a dip in a freezing river or even starting a campfire when you have no tools. All the tips and information has been researched and proven through many outdoorsmen's trials and efforts in God's great wilderness. Take a moment during your daily devotions and look through the guide to find information that will assist you in your journey. Take the guide with you in your backpack and use it as a survival guide.

The devotions found here are based on the classical method of lectio divina: reading, thinking, praying, and living Scripture with the intention of inviting an infinite, omniscient God into your life — as it is, no gloss, no veneer. Lectio divina is more Bible basking than Bible study, as it teaches you to absorb and meditate on Scripture, to converse with God openly, and to live out what has become a part of you — his Word. When you have finished the devotions, share this trail guide with a friend, hunting companion, or someone who loves the outdoors. Use it as an opportunity to cast your bread upon the waters.

This guide will provide helpful information to make your outdoor adventure more pleasant, and the Scripture and devotions will be a great way to start your day in the presence of God. We understand that we may have but just a moment to touch a life, and for that reason, we are guided to demonstrate an unselfish, supernatural hope and the life transformation that comes with that hope.

With your purchase of this trail guide, a portion of the proceeds will be donated to ELEVÁRE International to continue to reach around the world, offering hope and elevating lives.

To learn more about the conservation of life and the conservation of the great outdoors, go to NavPress.com, MossyOak.com, and ElevareInternational.com.

See you on the trail,

Barry Sneed
Executive Vice President, NavPress
General Editor

At Mossy Oak and Mossy Oak Nativ Nurseries one of our passions is making the environment a better place for the next generation. Mr. Fox, Neil, Daniel, and Toxey Haas are involved in this process from the acorn to the mighty oak tree. At Mossy Oak it is not just a tradition, it is a passion.

SURVIVAL PHILOSOPHY

The Colorado Department of Natural Resources promotes the following tips for planning for wilderness survival:

- Always maintain a positive attitude, reaffirming to yourself that you will survive.
- Tell someone where you are going and when you will return.
- Take someone with you. Never go alone.
- Have a plan, and stick to it. Stay put if you are lost or stranded, unless it becomes evident that self-rescue is the only option.
- Always carry a survival kit and first aid kit, and know how to use them.
- Dress for the weather, but be prepared for changes.
- Always carry raingear. Protection from the elements must be your priority.
- Practice S.T.O.P.:

    S — Sit down and stay put until the fear and rush of emotions has subsided.

    T — Think through your situation. What do you have available? What needs to be done?

    O — Observe your surroundings. Where should you stay? Will someone know you are missing? How long before you will be missed? If searchers are likely to be looking for you, is there an open place where you can be spotted more easily?

    P — Plan your action. Priorities might be: shelter, fire, signal, water, or find your way out to safety.

- Never quit!

A SURVIVAL MENTALITY

Here are a few survival stories that illustrate the benefit of having a survival mentality.

Randy Knapp, at eighteen years old, with two teenage friends, decided to summit Mount Hood on New Year's Day. Equipped with appropriate supplies for ten days, Randy and his friends were doing well until they were hit by a blinding snowstorm and decided to head home. Having left their map in the truck, they mistakenly headed in the wrong direction and were lost in the snowstorm. They spent the next thirteen nights, for a total of sixteen, in a snow cave before they crawled out and were spotted by searchers.

Colby Coombs, twenty-five years old, was vacationing in the Alaska Range in June 1992. He and his two climbing friends were caught in an avalanche on Mount Foraker. They were knocked 800 feet down the mountain. Coombs was knocked unconscious and woke up six hours later, dangling from his rope.

He had sustained a fractured ankle, a broken shoulder blade, and two broken vertebrae in his neck. His two friends did not survive the avalanche. The next four days, he struggled to climb down to their base camp and then traverse another five miles to cross the Kahiltna Glacier before being rescued.

Here is what he said about his survival: "If you get in trouble, anything that gets in the way of success has to be eliminated — emotion, fear, pain. It's the mental things that will impede your survival."

Amy Racina, on day twelve of a seventeen-day solo trek through King's Canyon National Park in California, was knocked down when a hillside crumbled beneath her. She fell sixty feet into a ravine, broke her hip, and shattered both legs in several places. She was twenty-five miles from the nearest trailhead and was not expected back for five more days. She dragged herself with her hands down the ravine for the next three days before being found by another hiker. It was another twenty-four hours after that before she was flown to safety.

Her thoughts on her survival: "The chances that I would get out of that ravine alive were very slim, but I never allowed myself to focus on the likelihood that I would die."

NOTES

_____

_____

_____

_____

THE SKEPTIC AND THE BELIEVER

PROVERBS 30:1-9

1-2 The skeptic swore, "There is no God!
   No God! — I can do anything I want!
I'm more animal than human;
   so-called human intelligence escapes me.

3-4 "I flunked 'wisdom.'
   I see no evidence of a holy God.
Has anyone ever seen Anyone
   climb into Heaven and take charge?
   grab the winds and control them?
   gather the rains in his bucket?
   stake out the ends of the earth?
Just tell me his name, tell me the names of his sons.
   Come on now — tell me!"

5-6 The believer replied, "Every promise of God proves true;
   he protects everyone who runs to him for help.
So don't second-guess him;
   he might take you to task and show up your lies."

7-9 And then he prayed, "God, I'm asking for two things
   before I die; don't refuse me —
Banish lies from my lips
   and liars from my presence.
Give me enough food to live on,
   neither too much nor too little.
If I'm too full, I might get independent,
   saying, 'God? Who needs him?'
If I'm poor, I might steal
   and dishonor the name of my God."

READ

As you read the words of this passage, be aware of the parts of your heart that are represented by the words. Perhaps under certain circumstances, you have intentionally ignored God's rules, while at other times you have run to God for protection, knowing he would help you.

THINK/PRAY

Read the passage a few more times. Each time you read, narrow your focus to the part that most deeply touches the reality of your life. Mull that over. Explore with God what he is saying to you through it, how he may want to lead, challenge, or refresh you.

LIVE

The prayer of verse 9 acknowledges the relationship between our physical and spiritual selves: When full of food, we may feel a false sense of security and disregard our need for God. When hungry, we may feel our need yet doubt that God will meet it.

Consider fasting today, for part or all of the day. Give up food or drink, or perhaps something you enjoy, such as reading or watching television. (Be sure to do this when you'll have time to replace your fasted activity with prayer. Also, check with your doctor before fasting from food or drink.) Let your fast help you get in touch with your heart's reaction to God.

When you would normally engage in the activity you're fasting from or when you feel an emptiness that you normally wouldn't notice, prayerfully read verse 9. In what ways does your fasting experience show you your need for God? Can you trust him to provide for your needs, or is your impulse to try to provide for yourself?

BASIC SURVIVAL KIT

A basic survival kit can be as diverse as the outdoor activities available. Use the following guidelines in developing the best survival kit for your needs and context of use.

When building your survival kit, consider layering. That is, think in layers:

- First Layer
  - Always with you
  - Small tin, waterproof container
  - Easy to attach or carry on your body (pocket-sized container, soft belt pouch, fanny pack)
- Second Layer
  - Larger items and additional items
  - Contained in a daypack or backpack
- Third Layer
  - Items that can be left at your base camp or vehicle
  - Plastic storage box, footlocker, and so forth

The more you think about it, the bigger your survival kit can grow, so this layering system will help you to prioritize and organize your equipment.

Basic survival categories with possible minimal items:

- Water
  - Purification tablets
  - Sponge
  - Water treatment filter straw
  - Small drip bottle containing household bleach (two to three drops per quart of water, plus thirty minutes for purification)
  - Plastic bags or a similar container for transporting water
- Fire
  - Lighter
  - Waterproof matches

- Candle
- Magnifying glass
- Shelter
  - 550 parachute cord
  - Large knife
  - Poncho
  - Space blanket
  - Wire saw
- Food
  - Knife
  - Snare wire
  - Fishhooks
  - Fishing and snare line
  - Bouillon cubes
  - High-energy food bars
  - Aluminum foil
  - Ziplock freezer bags
- Medical
  - Diarrhea medication
  - Surgical blades
  - Suture kit
  - Butterfly Band-Aids
  - Ibuprofen
  - Antibiotic cream
  - Surgical blades
  - Safety pins
- Signal
  - Signaling mirror
  - Glow sticks (can be attached to string and swung overhead at night and are highly visible to searching aircraft)
  - Loud whistle
  - Mini LED light with extra battery
- Navigation
  - Compass
  - Map
  - GPS with extra batteries
- Miscellaneous and Multipurpose
  - Duct tape
  - Pen or pencil and paper
  - Sewing thread and needle

GOD, BRILLIANT LORD

PSALM 8

1   GOD, brilliant Lord,
        yours is a household name.

2   Nursing infants gurgle choruses about you;
        toddlers shout the songs
That drown out enemy talk,
        and silence atheist babble.

3-4   I look up at your macro-skies, dark and enormous,
        your handmade sky-jewelry,
Moon and stars mounted in their settings.
        Then I look at my micro-self and wonder,
Why do you bother with us?
        Why take a second look our way?

5-8   Yet we've so narrowly missed being gods,
        bright with Eden's dawn light.
You put us in charge of your handcrafted world,
        repeated to us your Genesis-charge,
Made us lords of sheep and cattle,
        even animals out in the wild,
Birds flying and fish swimming,
        whales singing in the ocean deeps.

9   GOD, brilliant Lord,
        your name echoes around the world.

READ

Read the passage aloud slowly.

THINK

Read the passage aloud again, letting your mouth play with the phrases, connections, and comparisons that appeal to you. Perhaps one of these does:

- "gurgle choruses" and "atheist babble"
- "macro-skies" and "micro-self"
- "handcrafted world" and "Genesis-charge"
- "household name" and "brilliant Lord"

One by one, hold in your mind the words that stood out to you. Imagine their physical representation, how they relate to each other. For example, hear the sounds of babies drowning out atheists, see God's name (and presence and power) as ordinary as something in your house yet so brilliantly magnificent as to echo around the world. What do these comparisons have to do with your life?

PRAY

Consider the exercise you just did. What does it make you want to say to God? Words of admiration? Requests to be a good caretaker of the earth? Offer it to him.

LIVE

In the evening or early morning when the sky is dark, take this book and a flashlight outside and read this psalm to God. Even if you have to whisper to avoid being heard, put your heart into it. Revel in the moment and enjoy God.

SHELTER

When considering emergency shelter, first apply these basic guidelines and then decide on the appropriate shelter:

- Look for something that is already made or that can function with little effort as an emergency shelter.
- Prepare the first night's shelter to just beyond minimum. You can always improve it later, and in a survival situation, there will be many other things that may need your attention and energy.
- Do not overexert yourself when building a shelter. Minimize perspiration water loss and spent energy.
- You will need to sleep as much as possible the first night in order to have the recovery and strength needed to execute the remainder of your survival plan.
- Level of shelter construction.
  - Off-the-ground: helps to guard against flash flood, heavy insects, and other animal problems.
  - On-the-ground: typically better than an in-ground shelter and less likely to flood. Insects prefer holes. The ground is colder and more moist if you dig into it.
  - In-ground: best when used in excruciating hot or cold conditions. In the desert, the sand will be cooler below the surface. In snow, digging a snow cave or a mere trench can take advantage of the snow's insulating properties.

SHELTER OPTIONS
- Snow Tree Pit
  - Find a tree with thick branches that can provide overhead cover.
  - Dig the snow out from around the tree trunk to the desired depth or until you reach ground.
  - Pack snow around the top and inside of the hole for support.
  - Place cut evergreen boughs over the top of the pit and place boughs in the bottom of the pit for insulation.

- Snow Trench
  - Designed to get you below the snow and wind level.
  - Takes advantage of snow's insulating factor.
  - Compacted snow may be cut into snow blocks and used as overhead covering.
  - If you are unable to make snow blocks, a poncho or other material may be used for a covering.
  - Build only one entrance and use your backpack or snow blocks as a door.
- One-Man A-Frame
  - Use three poles (one 12-foot long and two 9-foot long).
  - Secure the long pole to a tree at about waist height.
  - Lay the two shorter poles on the ground, one on each side of and parallel to the long pole.
  - Lay your tarp or other shelter material over the long pole so that equal amounts of material hang from both sides.
  - Tuck the excess material under the short poles and spread on the ground inside to serve as a floor.
  - Stake down or place a pole between the two short poles to keep the shelter's entrance from being pulled inward.
- A-Frame Poncho Tent
- No-Pole Tepee
  - Tie a line to the top of your tepee material.
  - Throw the line over a tree limb and tie it to the tree trunk.
  - Starting at the opposite side from the door, begin to stake down the material.
  - Tie the tepee material to the stake material.
  - After staking down the material, adjust the suspension line to tighten the tepee material and retie it to the tree trunk.
- Lean-To
  - The lower the support rope or branch, the lower the potential for heat loss.
  - To reduce heat loss to the ground, place some type of insulating material, such as leaves or pine needles, inside the lean-to.
  - As much as 80 percent of body heat may be lost to the ground.
  - This design can be improved with the addition of a fire reflector.
  - Tie a six-foot pole to two trees, from waist to chest height. If two trees are not available, improvise by using Y-shaped sticks or tripods.

- Place one end of the beams (nine-foot poles) on one side of the horizontal support.
- Place the backside of the shelter into the wind.
- Crisscross saplings or vines on the beams.
- Cover the framework with brush, leaves, pine needles, or grass, starting at the bottom and working your way up.
- Fire Reflector
  - Drive four long stakes into the ground to support the wall.
  - Stack green logs on top of one another between the support stakes to make the wall.
  - Improvement: Form two rows of stacked logs to create an inner space within the wall that you can fill with dirt. This action will not only strengthen the wall but also will make it more heat reflective.
  - Bind the top of the support stakes to keep the logs in place.

NOTES

A SAFE PLACE TO HIDE

PSALM 46:3-11

3   Jacob-wrestling God fights for us,
          GOD-of-Angel-Armies protects us.

4-6   River fountains splash joy, cooling God's city,
          this sacred haunt of the Most High.
    God lives here, the streets are safe,
          God at your service from crack of dawn.
    Godless nations rant and rave, kings and kingdoms threaten,
          but Earth does anything he says.

7   Jacob-wrestling God fights for us,
          GOD-of-Angel-Armies protects us.

8-10 Attention, all! See the marvels of GOD!
          He plants flowers and trees all over the earth,
    Bans war from pole to pole,
          breaks all the weapons across his knee.
    "Step out of the traffic! Take a long,
          loving look at me, your High God,
          above politics, above everything."

11   Jacob-wrestling God fights for us,
          GOD-of-Angel-Armies protects us.

READ

Read the passage aloud.

THINK

When have you felt the safest in your lifetime? Why? Circle or underline every word in this passage that deals with the concept of safety and security. Consider your emotions that rise up in response to the words of this passage.

Why do you think the psalmist repeats this phrase three times: "Jacob-wrestling God fights for us, God-of-Angel-Armies protects us"?

What would your life look like if you lived this out: "Step out of the traffic! Take a long, loving look at me, your High God, above politics, above everything"?

PRAY

Take several minutes to free your mind of every anxious thought, concern, or stress that you have. Ask God to release you from these thoughts that hold you captive and paralyze you.

After this time, ask God to fill you with the promises from this psalm concerning the safety and security found only in him.

LIVE

In the midst of your busy schedule today, live in the safety of God.

FIRE BUILDING

Remember the three primary elements of a fire, and you will have greater success in this area. All fires need air, heat, and fuel.

Location is the first item in fire building. Be sure to choose an area that offers protection from the wind and is relatively flat.

Fuel is the next consideration. Fuel can be divided into three categories, adding them at the appropriate time in order to build your fire gradually:

1. Tinder: ignited with a spark. Can be dry leaves; fine, dry grass; bark; dead evergreen needles; gunpowder; cotton lint; cloth fibers; spruce or pine resin; sawdust or straw; or even a bird's nest.
2. Kindling: small twigs, strips of wood. Added to tinder to build up the fire.
3. Fuel: branches and logs for sustained burning.

FIRE DESIGN AND FUNCTION
Choose a design that best suits your needs:

- Tepee: good for use with wet wood and for signal fire.
- Lean-to: may be the easiest fire to build.
- Pyramid: good for burning through the night with little attention.
- Cross ditch: useful for cooking. The shallow ditch allows for improved air circulation while keeping the fire lower and out of the wind. The ditches should be about six inches deep, and the intersection should be twelve to twenty-four inches wide.

FIRE IGNITION
1. Matches: Think one match = one fire.
2. Lighter.
3. Flint strike or metal match (produces a spark of 3,000°F).
4. Primitive methods:

- Fire Bow: most friction, least energy, most time to make.
  - Materials needed:
    - Flat-base board — sturdy, dry, and at least one inch thick.
    - Spindle stick, about one inch thick and straight, about twelve inches long.
    - Wooden block or spindle socket to press down on the top of the spindle. Should fit comfortably in the hand.
    - Bow — one inch thick, two-foot long green wood, strong but flexible. Needs to be able to support the downward pressure you will apply.
    - Long sturdy string — not less than six inches.
  - Technique:
    - Downward pressure is applied to the block while rotation of the spindle is achieved by moving the bow.
    - Place a leaf or similar material beneath the notch in order to catch the charred dust. This burning ember pile will be used to ignite your tinder piles.
    - Maintaining a consistent sawing motion will help create a charred build-up in the notch.
    - Continue to rotate the spindle on the baseboard until it begins to smoke or until the char dust ignites into an ember.
    - Using a leaf or other catch material, transfer the ember to your tinder bundle.
    - Blow into the tinder bundle to increase the oxygen supply to the ember, thus increasing the fire.
- Fire Plow: the least preparation and skill are needed with this method, but it is the most work. Use thick sticks.
  - Materials needed:
    - Plow stick, twelve to twenty-four inches long and at least two inches in diameter.
    - Base wood, which should be softer than the plow stick, if possible, and at least two inches wide.
    - Try to avoid woods with high resin content, as it can cause glazing and reduce friction.
    - The drier the wood, the better.
  - Technique:
    - Use the plow to make a groove (about six inches long) in the base wood.
    - Push back and forth to indent the groove.

- Place one hand about an inch above the tip of the plow to provide back and forth plowing movement, and place the other over the butt end to apply downward pressure.
- The secret is finding the right balance between pressure and speed.
- A fire plow is most effective if the balance between speed and pressure is maintained. If you get tired, switch off with a partner in order to keep the speed up.
- Once the groove is made, lower the end of the plow in order to increase the contact area between the plow and base.
- As the wood dries out from the friction of the plow motion, heat will begin to build up, and black dust will begin to form. Stop your downward plowing motion at the same spot in order to collect and form a dust pile that will become the ember.
- As the dust forms, raise the butt end of the plow and focus the heat on the tip.
- Continue the back and forth plowing motion, touching the accumulating dust at the end of the groove without collapsing the dust pile.
- Once you have a coal, transfer it to your tinder bundle and blow into a flame.

NOTES

NOT A SCORCH MARK

DANIEL 3:19-27

19-23 Nebuchadnezzar, his face purple with anger, cut off Shadrach, Meshach, and Abednego. He ordered the furnace fired up seven times hotter than usual. He ordered some strong men from the army to tie them up, hands and feet, and throw them into the roaring furnace. Shadrach, Meshach, and Abednego, bound hand and foot, fully dressed from head to toe, were pitched into the roaring fire. Because the king was in such a hurry and the furnace was so hot, flames from the furnace killed the men who carried Shadrach, Meshach, and Abednego to it, while the fire raged around Shadrach, Meshach, and Abednego.

24 Suddenly King Nebuchadnezzar jumped up in alarm and said, "Didn't we throw three men, bound hand and foot, into the fire?"

"That's right, O king," they said.

25 "But look!" he said. "I see four men, walking around freely in the fire, completely unharmed! And the fourth man looks like a son of the gods!"

26 Nebuchadnezzar went to the door of the roaring furnace and called in, "Shadrach, Meshach, and Abednego, servants of the High God, come out here!"

Shadrach, Meshach, and Abednego walked out of the fire.

27 All the important people, the government leaders and king's counselors, gathered around to examine them and discovered that the fire hadn't so much as touched the three men — not a hair singed, not a scorch mark on their clothes, not even the smell of fire on them!

READ

Read the passage aloud slowly.

THINK

Read the passage aloud again, but this time read the dialogue as theatrically as possible. Catch the incredulous tones of the king in verses 24-25. And in verse 26, call out loudly as the king did.

Now read the passage silently and let yourself become someone in the passage: a bystander watching it all, the king, one of the three men, or even the mysterious fourth man. Imagine the thoughts and feelings of the person whose role you have assumed. If you had been this person, how would this experience have affected your relationship with God?

PRAY

Respond to God from what has come to you in this passage — particularly about trusting in him.

LIVE

Sit quietly before God with the palms of your hands open and turned upward. Receive from God. Be particularly open to receiving guidance, just as Shadrach, Meshach, and Abednego received from God. Receive the courage he gave them. Receive the power he gave them.

FINDING WATER

WHERE TO LOOK
- Shaded areas.
- Muddy ground.
- Low-lying spots.
- Thick vegetation.
- At the base of a sand dune belt (especially large, steep ones).
- At the base of cliffs with moderate or dense vegetation.
- Morning dew (collect it with a towel, sponge, or clothing).
- Rainwater collected in sandstone ridges, canyons, or rocks.
- Animal tracks, circling birds, and insects will usually be found close to a water source.

WATER COLLECTION
- Dig where soil is damp. Keep digging until water seeps into it.
- Turn over half-buried stones in the desert just before dawn. Dew will form on the cooler surface.
- Prickly Pear cactus is safe to eat and contains a great deal of moisture.
- Snow and ice should be melted before consuming as a source of water. The reduced body temperature from eating snow or ice will lead to dehydration.
- Gray-colored sea ice or sea ice that is opaque is salty — do not use it if you cannot desalinate it.
- Bluish-colored sea ice has little salt in it.
- Sea water should not be consumed without desalination.
- Rainwater is more easily collected with a wide-mouth container.
  - A plastic tarp can be spread out with a hole made in the middle.
  - Place it above the ground with your water receptacle underneath the hole.
  - When no other container is available, water on the beach can be collected by digging deep enough to allow water to seep into the hole.

- ○ Build a fire and heat the rocks.
- ○ Drop the hot rocks into the water.
- ○ Hold a cloth or shirt above the steam and collect the potable water.

TREATING POTENTIAL DRINKING WATER
- Filtration
  - Does not purify.
  - Reduces particles and sediment to help water taste better.
- Boiling
  - The most certain method of killing microorganisms.
  - Will not neutralize chemical pollutants.
- Chemical
  - Use water purification tablets.
- Water purifier filter
  - Microbial purification filters remove parasites.
  - Kills waterborne bacteria and viruses.

SIMPLE WATER FILTER
1. Punch five to ten holes in the bottom of a water container. (Birch tree bark can be used as a funnel by rolling into a cone shape and tying it closed to keep it from unrolling.)
2. Place rocks, pebbles, cotton or some other material at the bottom of your container to prevent the sand from falling through the holes, yet still allow the water to pass through the holes.
3. Add a layer of gravel. This will prevent sand mixed with the water that you get through the filter.
4. Fill your water filter container with sand.
5. Collect water and pour through the filter material.
6. If the water is not clear, consider passing it through the filter more than once.
7. Your filtered water may be made safe to drink by adding a layer of charcoal between the gravel and the sand layer.
   - Gather the charcoal from your fire.
   - Crush it into gravel-size, not powder.

THE IMPORTANCE OF WORDS

PROVERBS 16:21-32

21   A wise person gets known for insight;
       gracious words add to one's reputation.

22   True intelligence is a spring of fresh water,
       while fools sweat it out the hard way.

23   They make a lot of sense, these wise folks;
       whenever they speak, their reputation increases.

24   Gracious speech is like clover honey —
       good taste to the soul, quick energy for the body.

25   There's a way that looks harmless enough;
       look again — it leads straight to hell.

26   Appetite is an incentive to work;
       hunger makes you work all the harder.

27   Mean people spread mean gossip;
       their words smart and burn.

28   Troublemakers start fights;
       gossips break up friendships.

29   Calloused climbers betray their very own friends;
       they'd stab their own grandmothers in the back.

30   A shifty eye betrays an evil intention;
       a clenched jaw signals trouble ahead.

31   Gray hair is a mark of distinction,
       the award for a God-loyal life.

32   Moderation is better than muscle,
       self-control better than political power.

READ

Read the passage. Underline the word or phrase that stands out to you the most. Read the passage again. Underline a different word or phrase that stands out to you.

THINK

You may have heard the saying that only two things cannot be taken back: time and our words. Think back over all the words you have said in conversation over the past twenty-four hours (conversations you have had with friends, comments you have made in passing, phone calls, jokes you have told, and so on). What percentage of your conversation would you say was positive, encouraging, and uplifting? What percentage was negative, discouraging, and sarcastic?

Consider the words you are glad you said. Consider the words you regret saying.

PRAY

For the words you regret, ask for forgiveness. For the positive words you spoke, thank God they were words that built up rather than tore down.

Ask God to bring to mind words of truth and healing that you could speak to others. Ask him to bring to mind specific people to whom you could speak these words in the next few days.

LIVE

Have the courage to seek out opportunities to speak words of truth and healing to people who need to hear them. Hold your tongue when you are upset or frustrated — when you are about to speak words you'll regret. Above all else, ask God to help you guard your mouth by thinking before speaking.

FINDING FOOD

Food is not the first priority in a survival situation, but it does have its place on a survival priority list.

OUTDOORSMAN'S SURVIVAL PRIORITY LIST
- Shelter
- Fire
- Water
- Food

Pound for pound and effort for effort, hunting and fishing will yield greater benefits for survival over gathering plants, as animal fat has a higher calorie potential than plant matter.

As a rule of thumb when considering a food source, be aware that 90 percent of plants are not edible for humans, while 90 percent of animal life is.

GENERAL POTENTIAL FOOD CATEGORIES
- Insects: easiest to catch, usually plentiful, good to eat.
  - Avoid fuzzy insects.
  - Cook or boil whenever possible.
- Frogs: easy to catch, nutritious.
- Reptiles: skin and cook thoroughly.
  - Snakes are difficult to catch and can be dangerous, but they are good to eat.
  - Lizards are hard to catch, but good to eat.
- Fish: most fish are good to eat.
- Birds and bird eggs: most are good to eat.
- Rabbits and deer can be an abundant food source. (Beware of sickly animals or those with a spotted liver. They may be carrying a disease and should not be consumed.)
- Cattails: good to eat.
- Roots and seeds: most are good to eat.
- Berries: 90 percent of purple, black, or blue berries are good to eat.

- Acorn nuts from North American Oak are edible, but they should be boiled (change the water several times) before consuming.
- Pine nuts: generally are good to eat, but some pine trees are poisonous.
- Plants that smell of onion or garlic are usually safe to eat.
- Cacti: mostly edible.
- Yucca flowers and stalks: edible.
- Seaweed and most green plants from the sea can be eaten.
- Dandelion roots, heads, and leaves are edible (discard the stem).

PLANTS TO AVOID
- Mushrooms.
- Shiny-leafed plants.
- Yellow and white berries.
- Red berries: Just as many are dangerous as there are safe species, so unless you are sure, it is better to avoid them.
- Umbrella-shaped flowers.
- Plants with three-leafed structures.
- Plants with milky sap.
- Grains are usually too much work to make them worth your time.
- Plants with an almond smell are usually poisonous.

NOTES

THE BREAD GOD HAS GIVEN

EXODUS 16:9-16

9   Moses instructed Aaron: "Tell the whole company of Israel: 'Come near to GOD. He's heard your complaints.'"

10   When Aaron gave out the instructions to the whole company of Israel, they turned to face the wilderness. And there it was: the Glory of GOD visible in the Cloud.

11-12   GOD spoke to Moses, "I've listened to the complaints of the Israelites. Now tell them: 'At dusk you will eat meat and at dawn you'll eat your fill of bread; and you'll realize that I am GOD, *your* God.'"

13-15   That evening quail flew in and covered the camp and in the morning there was a layer of dew all over the camp. When the layer of dew had lifted, there on the wilderness ground was a fine flaky something, fine as frost on the ground. The Israelites took one look and said to one another, *man-hu* (What is it?). They had no idea what it was.

15-16   So Moses told them, "It's the bread GOD has given you to eat. And these are GOD's instructions: 'Gather enough for each person, about two quarts per person; gather enough for everyone in your tent.'"

READ

Read the passage aloud. Have fun pronouncing *man-hu* in different ways. If you'd like, read the expanded passage to get a picture of the complaining that came before this and the obsessive hoarding that came after. Both give us a picture of the neediness of the Israelites at this time.

THINK

Read the passage again slowly, pausing to feel each emotion of the Israelites:

- the deep neediness of complaining
- the excitement of seeing the glory of God visible in the Cloud
- the perplexity of seeing this strange bread from heaven
- the satisfaction of having enough

Then consider: If you were to complain to God right now, what would your complaint be? (Don't choose this yourself; wait and let it come to you.) In what ways, if any, have you been perplexed by God's response to your complaining? How might God have truly provided enough but you didn't recognize it as God's bread from heaven — exactly what you needed?

PRAY

If you haven't formally complained to God about this matter, do so. Ask God to show you how he has provided you with enough, even though you still might wonder.

LIVE

Sit in the quiet and feel God's "enoughness" in your body. Where do you feel it? In arms that are full? In a quiet mind? In a stomach that feels full? In muscles that work well? If you can really mean it, try delighting in this enoughness.

SIGNALING FOR HELP

When signaling for help, remember the general rule of three:

- Three of something signifies that help is needed.
- Three whistle blasts:
  - Blow three distinct times, then wait three to five minutes and repeat three blasts.
  - Continue every fifteen minutes.
- Three gun shots.
- Three piles of dark wood on light sand.
- Three fires burning, arranged in a triangle pattern.

ATTRACTING GROUND SEARCHERS
- Smoke
- Note
- Whistle
- Signs using rocks, branches
- Display clothing or equipment
- Gunshots

ATTRACTING AIR SEARCHERS
- Smoke
- Mirror
- Clothing

ATTRACTING MARINE SEARCHERS
- Flares
- Radio
- Mirror
- Maintain a high profile in the water
- Stay near the wreckage
- Flags, clothing

CLOTHING

- Spread on the ground or on top of a tree.
- Use bright colors if available.

NATURAL MATERIAL

- Use natural materials to spell out SOS.
- In snow-covered areas, tramp down the snow to form letters and fill in with contrasting material such as twigs or dirt.
- In sand, use vegetation.

If your signal is acknowledged by an aircraft and understood, the pilot will rock the aircraft from side to side (during the day or moonlight) or will make green flashes with the plane's signal lamp (at night).

If your signal is received but not understood, the aircraft will make a complete circle (during the day or moonlight) or will make red flashes with its signal lamp (at night).

BODY SIGNALS

- Both arms raised with palms open means "I need help."
- One arm raised with palm open means "I do not need help."

NOTES

I WILL ANSWER YOU

JEREMIAH 33:2-3

2-3 "This is GOD's Message, the God who made earth, made it livable and lasting, known everywhere as *GOD*: 'Call to me and I will answer you. I'll tell you marvelous and wondrous things that you could never figure out on your own.'"

READ

Find a quiet place and read this passage slowly. Pause in the silence. Let these words wash over you. Make them personal. Claim them as God speaking specifically to you.

THINK

What sticks out to you? What word or phrase settles deeply in your soul? Why?

Deep down, do you really believe that God will answer you when you call to him? Why or why not? What does this passage say about his character?

As you hear God's personal message, spoken straight from his being, what do you feel? What words from this passage can you make your own?

PRAY

Ask God what he wants you to do with the word or phrase he has given you. Ask him how you can best live out this gift that the Holy Spirit has placed before you. Listen patiently in the silence for the response. You may be tempted to move on to some other thought or task, but resist, simply resting in the silence yet listening actively.

LIVE

Go and live out the answer of what the Holy Spirit instructed you to do today.

FIRST AID TIPS

Sooner or later in the outdoors, you will have to manage an injury. Knowledge and preparedness are your keys to success. Consider packing these basic first aid kit items for one to two people on a one- to seven-day trip.

BANDAGES
- Ten one-inch sterile strips
- Five four-by-four-inch sterile pads
- Five non-adherent pads
- Four gauze rolls (three-inch)
- Four PolyMem dressings (one-inch)
- Two PolyMem dressings (two-inch)
- Two Steri-strips skin closures (packet of three)

BLISTERS AND SPRAINS
- Four medicated blister pads
- One elastic bandage (three-inch)
- Two moleskin pads
- One Molefoam pad

BURNS, RASHES, AND STINGS
- Two tubes burn cream (two ounces)
- One tube hydrocortisone cream
- One insect sting relief medication
- One moist burn pad
- One Tegaderm dressing (four-inch)

WOUND CARE
- Ten cotton balls
- Four iodine prep pads
- One tube of triple antibiotic cream
- Two tubes of super glue
- Two bottles of surgical soap (four-ounce squeeze bottles)
- One roll of adhesive tape (one inch by ten feet)

DENTAL
- Temporary filling material

GLOVES
- Two pairs of latex-free examination gloves

CPR MASK

EYE, NOSE, AND THROAT
- One sterile eye pad
- One saline nasal spray
- Three tongue depressors

INSTRUMENTS
- Six safety pins
- One SAM splint
- One pair of scissors
- One tick remover tool and pair of tweezers

NON-RX MEDICATION
- Eight acetaminophen packets (two-tab packets)
- Eight ibuprofen packets (two-tab packets)

SURVIVAL BLANKET

ABC OF FIRST AID

Your general knowledge and first aid practices, along with CPR skills, should reflect the intensity of your outdoor activities and take into consideration the level of extremity of those activities.

If an emergency does occur, apply the ABC of first aid (Airway, Breathing, and Circulation) until professional medical care arrives. When using the ABC of first aid, the first thing to do is check the patient's airway. If the patient is unconscious, very carefully lift his or her chin and tilt the head back. Sweep the back of the mouth with a finger to check for obstructions if you suspect a blockage.

Next, check for breathing. Place your face close to the patient's mouth to listen and feel for air, or put a mirror next to the patient's mouth to see if condensation builds up. If the patient is not breathing, administer rescue breathing and CPR until he or she is breathing again.

Finally, circulation should be checked by monitoring the patient's pulse at the wrist or throat. Also, assess the patient's color; if he or she is pale or splotchy, circulation is likely compromised. Try to keep the patient warm, and apply pressure to obvious sites of bleeding.

NOTES

GIVING COMFORT

JOB 5:17-21

17-19   "So, what a blessing when God steps in and corrects you!
    Mind you, don't despise the discipline of Almighty God!
True, he wounds, but he also dresses the wound;
    the same hand that hurts you, heals you.
From one disaster after another he delivers you;
    no matter what the calamity, the evil can't touch you —

20-21   "In famine, he'll keep you from starving,
    in war, from being gutted by the sword.
You'll be protected from vicious gossip
    and live fearless through any catastrophe."

READ

Read the passage aloud slowly, keeping in mind that Eliphaz from Teman is speaking to his friend Job, who has just experienced the death of his children and the loss of all he had.

THINK

Read the passage again and put yourself in the place of Job, who listened to these words. How do they fall on your ear?

Read the passage again and put yourself in the place of Eliphaz. What feelings and attitudes fill you as you speak these words?

1. What makes a comforter really helpful? Is telling the truth enough?
2. What did Job need from Eliphaz?
3. What might be in the heart of a person who preaches at someone who is so far down?

PRAY

Ask the Comforter, the Holy Spirit, to give you what is needed to truly comfort despairing people. If you want guidance for your prayer, ask the Comforter to give you tools to help people in trouble go to him. Ask him to give you tools to draw them out to say to him whatever they need to express. Plead with the Comforter to make you his messenger, to prevent you from moralizing and giving advice.

LIVE

Rest your mind on someone who is in deep trouble. Pray only the word *peace* for them — no suggestions, no fixing, no rescuing. Just trusting.

BLISTER CARE TIPS

It begins with a hot spot, and if not managed correctly, it can evolve into a debilitating blister.

Prevention is the best measure for avoiding blisters. Heat, moisture, and friction are the primary elements necessary for promoting the development of a blister. Moisture-wicking socks, single- or double-layered, can be of great assistance. Also, drying powders like talcum power or the use of petroleum jelly as a lubricant have proven to be helpful, depending on the length of time in your footwear. Even duct tape has been used with great success.

When blisters appear, here are some suggestions on how to manage this painful situation:

- First, try not to open the blister. As long as it has not popped, it is safe from infection.
- Apply a second skin or moleskin around the hot spot to help relieve pressure and reduce the friction.
- If the blister does burst, treat it as any other open wound, managing the area to help prevent infection.
- Try to always leave large blisters intact.
- To help drain larger blisters, use a sterile, threaded needle and pass the thread through the blister, leaving the ends of the thread sticking out of the blister. This will allow for continued drainage, as the thread acts as a wick for the discharge.
- After complete draining and relief has been secured, the thread can be removed. Seal the small holes with a liquid bandage. In the meantime, keep the area clean and covered to reduce the chance of further irritation.

DEALING WITH DEHYDRATION

Dying of thirst can be a very real statement in a survival situation. The human body can only survive a few days without water. Dehydration can happen quickly in hot conditions, but it is possible in any climate, as our bodies lose moisture through perspiration, feces, urine, and even our breath.

Every cell, organ, and function in the human body requires water, and dehydration is a condition that can be brought about in a matter of hours — not just days — and is a serious condition beyond just being thirsty.

Watch for these increasingly dangerous signs of dehydration:

- Serious case of "cotton mouth" and infrequent urination with low output. Your urine will have a darker color and a stronger odor than normal.
- If not treated, your dehydration will continue to worsen and your urination will be even less. Your eyes will become dry and look sunken as they are robbed of moisture. Your heart rate will become elevated.
- Severe dehydration has set in when urination has ceased. You become lethargic, irritable, and nauseous. Vomiting usually will accompany this stage, further hastening your complete dehydration. If you fail to rehydrate at this stage, your body could fall into a state of shock as major organs begin to shut down, followed by death.

Once water is secured, begin drinking slowly and resist the impulse to guzzle. Drinking too quickly can increase your nausea and vomiting. Avoid alcohol and caffeine, as they can act as diuretics. Do not drink salt water! This will only worsen your dehydrated state.

BLESSING GOD

PSALM 103:1-14

1-2   O my soul, bless GOD.
     From head to toe, I'll bless his holy name!
   O my soul, bless GOD,
     don't forget a single blessing!

3-5   He forgives your sins — every one.
   He heals your diseases — every one.
   He redeems you from hell — saves your life!
   He crowns you with love and mercy — a paradise crown.
   He wraps you in goodness — beauty eternal.
   He renews your youth — you're always young in his presence.

6-14   GOD makes everything come out right;
     he puts victims back on their feet.
   He showed Moses how he went about his work,
     opened up his plans to all Israel.
   GOD is sheer mercy and grace;
     not easily angered, he's rich in love.
   He doesn't endlessly nag and scold,
     nor hold grudges forever.
   He doesn't treat us as our sins deserve,
     nor pay us back in full for our wrongs.
   As high as heaven is over the earth,
     so strong is his love to those who fear him.
   And as far as sunrise is from sunset,
     he has separated us from our sins.
   As parents feel for their children,
     GOD feels for those who fear him.
   He knows us inside and out,
     keeps in mind that we're made of mud.

READ

Read the passage quietly to yourself.

THINK

The idea of blessing God may sound odd to us. We might think, *Who am I to bless God? Isn't God the only one to bless people?* But the literal meaning of the Hebrew word *bless* is "to kneel."* So when we bless God, our souls kneel to him, usually in worship or gratitude.

Read the passage again with your heart kneeling before God. If possible, physically kneel where you are and read aloud. As you do, notice the phrases that reflect what you are most eager to praise God for — perhaps that he isn't easily angered or doesn't endlessly nag.

PRAY

Stay kneeling and pray aloud those phrases about God that touched you most. As you pray, add to them other ideas about God that come to mind. Raise your hands if you wish.

LIVE

Quietly kneel before God in whatever posture and mood this psalm has brought you:

- resting peacefully on your heels with your hands in your lap
- rising onto your knees with your hands raised
- kneeling before a chair or bed and bringing your whole self forward onto it

Be with God this way for a few minutes.

---

* W. E. Vine, *An Expository Dictionary of Biblical Words*, eds. Merrill F. Unger and William White (Nashville: Thomas Nelson, 1985), 18.

DEALING WITH DIARRHEA

In an outdoor setting, diarrhea actually can become a very dangerous condition that can quickly lead to dehydration, a potentially life-threatening situation.

Typically this aliment can be caused by a change in water or food and also from ingesting contaminated water or spoiled food, poor hygiene, and improper utensil cleaning. Fatigue also can hasten this problem.

Boiling your water and good hygiene practices can help to avoid this issue. But should it attack you, be sure to treat it seriously. If you have not included an over-the-counter medicine like Pepto-Bismol, Imodium A-D, or Kaopectate in your first aid supplies, think about including one of these items.

But what if you forgot these convenient meds or your buddy has used them all up and now you need them? What can you do? Burn a log. A burned log actually can help relieve this uncomfortable problem. Scrape the black charcoal from the burned log and mix it with clean water. Drink small amounts of this liquid every two hours until the diarrhea subsides.

NOTES

SELF-EXAMINATION

PROVERBS 10:22-32

22   God's blessing makes life rich;
        nothing we do can improve on God.

23   An empty-head thinks mischief is fun,
        but a mindful person relishes wisdom.

24   The nightmares of the wicked come true;
        what the good people desire, they get.

25   When the storm is over, there's nothing left of the wicked;
        good people, firm on their rock foundation, aren't even fazed.

26   A lazy employee will give you nothing but trouble;
        it's vinegar in the mouth, smoke in the eyes.

27   The Fear-of-God expands your life;
        a wicked life is a puny life.

28   The aspirations of good people end in celebration;
        the ambitions of bad people crash.

29   God is solid backing to a well-lived life,
        but he calls into question a shabby performance.

30   Good people *last* — they can't be moved;
        the wicked are here today, gone tomorrow.

31   A good person's mouth is a clear fountain of wisdom;
        a foul mouth is a stagnant swamp.

32   The speech of a good person clears the air;
        the words of the wicked pollute it.

READ

Stand in front of a mirror and read the passage. When you're finished, stand motionless. Stare at yourself in the mirror.

THINK

When we read passages of God's Message that speak about the unrighteous or the evil or foolish person, we are often reminded of other individuals and think to ourselves, *That certainly isn't talking about me.* But we must be careful not to be blinded by the sin and pride in our own lives. Take a few minutes to perform a thorough self-examination. (This might be a difficult exercise for you; being willing to see our true selves is not easy.)

PRAY

Reread the passage. After each verse, pause, look in the mirror, and whisper, "God, is this me?" Allow time for God to prompt truths in your heart. Some of these thoughts may be hard to hear. If God brings to mind specific areas where you have failed, ask him to forgive you. If God brings to mind areas where you can grow, ask him to help you mature as you follow him. If God brings to mind ways in which you are living faithfully, thank him for his grace in your life.

LIVE

Whatever God-honoring quality was revealed to you today as you asked the question, "God, is this me?" go and live in that manner.

FROSTBITE

This can be a serious medical condition involving localized damage to skin and other tissue due to extreme cold or prolonged exposure to cold. Frostbite typically occurs in small areas on extremities of the body such as fingers, toes, ears, and nose.

Frostbite can be brought on by overexposure to cold, wet conditions at or below 32°F or with wind chills below freezing. It should be noted that air temperatures do not have to be below freezing to have the potential for frostbite. Wet skin or clothing on a windy day also can lead to frostbite.

STAGES OF FROSTBITE
- Frostnip
    - Ice crystals form in the tissues but no tissue destruction occurs, as the ice crystals quickly dissolve when the skin is warmed.
    - Usually affects earlobes, cheeks, nose, fingers, and toes.
    - The skin will be pale, and numbness or tingling occurs until warmed.
- Superficial Frostbite (first- and second-degree frostbite)
    - Affected area feels cold, usually numb.
    - Clumsiness.
    - Skin turns white or yellow.
    - Severe pain with rewarming.
- Deep Frostbite (third- and fourth-degree frostbite)
    - All of the above characteristics, plus deep, blood-filled blisters.
    - Infection is a higher risk at this stage.
    - Blackened skin.
    - Fourth degree can penetrate all skin layers and can begin to affect muscle tissue, tendons, nerves, and bones.

TREATMENT FOR FROSTBITE
- Elevate the body part to help reduce swelling.
- Move to a warm area to prevent further heat loss.

- Avoid walking on frostbitten feet to minimize further damage.
- Check for hypothermia, as many times these two conditions are presented together. If so, treat the hypothermia first.
- Remove all jewelry and wet and constrictive clothing. These can hinder blood flow and promote continued heat loss.
- Give the person warm, nonalcoholic, non-caffeinated fluids or broths to drink.
- Keep the injured part away from sources of heat until professional treatment can be secured, offering proper rewarming techniques.
- Do not rub affected skin. Friction will cause further tissue damage.

PREVENTING FROSTBITE

Prevention, as always, is the best treatment:

- Always wear climate and activity-appropriate clothing.
- Clothing should be loose-fitting and layered.
- Keep hands, feet, and head covered.
- Outer clothing should be wind- and water-resistant.
- Remove wet clothing and footwear as soon as possible, and replace it with dry gear.
- Alcohol and many drugs can accelerate the effects of cold on the body.

NOTES

HYPOTHERMIA

Hypothermia is the physical condition of the body's core temperature dropping below 95°F (35°C). This physical state can be life-threatening and progress slowly, and thus not be recognized until perhaps it is too late. It is important, therefore, to know and identify the stages of hypothermia and deal with each one appropriately.

Wearing wet or inadequate clothing, falling into cold water, or even not covering your head in cold weather can heighten the chances of hypothermia.

STAGE 1
- Your body's temperature will drop 2–3°F (1–2°C) below normal.
- You will begin to shiver, and your hands may begin to feel numb.
- The blood vessels are starting to constrict, thus limiting the use of your extremities.
- Goose bumps may be present.

STAGE 2
- A feeling of "warming" back up will signal entering this stage, but you remain cold.
- You will struggle to touch your thumb to your little finger or be unable to perform this simple task at all.
- Your body temperature has now dropped 3–7°F (2–4°C) below normal.
- You may notice that your extremities are beginning to turn blue.

STAGE 3
- Your body is now at the limit of its ability to continue to function, and more cellular functions will begin to shut down.
- This will be evident by greater areas of your body turning blue.
- If this is not soon managed, the major organs of your body will begin to fail, thus ushering in an imminent death.

Being able to recognize the seriousness of these stages, knowing what can be done, and being educated will allow you to monitor your warmth and allow you to initiate strategies to guard your overall state of health.

Monitor these signs and take these steps promoted by the Mayo Clinic for managing hypothermia.

SIGNS OF HYPOTHERMIA

- Shivering
- Slurred speech
- Abnormally slow breathing
- Cool, pale skin
- Loss of coordination

CARE FOR HYPOTHERMIA

- Monitor the person's breathing. If it stops, begin CPR immediately.
- Move the person out of the cold. If going indoors is not possible, then protect the person from the wind, cover his head, and insulate his body from the cold ground.
- Remove wet clothing, and provide dry covering.
- Do not apply direct heat. Do not directly use hot water. Instead, apply warm compresses to the center of the body: the neck, chest, and groin. Do not attempt to warm the arms and legs. Heat applied to the arms and legs will force cold blood back toward the heart, lungs, and brain, thus causing the core temperature to continue to fall. This can be FATAL.
- Do not give the person alcohol. Offer warm, nonalcoholic drinks, unless the person is vomiting.
- Do not try to reheat by rubbing or massaging the person. His or her skin may be frostbitten, and rubbing frostbitten tissue can cause severe damage.

NOTES

CELEBRATING GOD

PSALM 34:1-9

1   I bless GOD every chance I get;
    my lungs expand with his praise.

2   I live and breathe GOD;
    if things aren't going well, hear this and be happy:

3   Join me in spreading the news;
    together let's get the word out.

4   GOD met me more than halfway,
    he freed me from my anxious fears.

5   Look at him; give him your warmest smile.
    Never hide your feelings from him.

6   When I was desperate, I called out,
    and GOD got me out of a tight spot.

7   GOD's angel sets up a circle
    of protection around us while we pray.

8   Open your mouth and taste, open your eyes and see —
        how good GOD is.
    Blessed are you who run to him.

9   Worship GOD if you want the best;
    worship opens doors to all his goodness.

READ

Read the passage aloud as many times as it takes for the words and thoughts to become familiar to you.

THINK/PRAY

Imagine the face and posture of the psalmist expressing this worship. Maybe you'd like to join him, or maybe you're annoyed. What posture does your body take on when you hear the speaker's enthusiasm? When you imagine the God he's speaking about? Move your body into this posture—be it bowing on the floor, clenching your fists, hugging your knees, folding your arms across your chest, dancing, or something else.

Now set aside your physical response and return to the text. Mull the words until you can determine your mental reaction to them. Can you put clear words to your thoughts? Tell God, and write them down.

Now return to the text one last time. Read it silently, listening for God's response to your posture and your words.

LIVE

In his book *Prayer,* Richard Foster speaks of stepping-stones along the path of learning to adore God. Ultimately, adoring God involves gratitude, magnifying him, and "foot-stomping celebration," but these must be grown into, and our hearts must be taught. A good first step is simply to make a habit of watching small things in nature: ducks, butterflies, fluttering leaves. This does not mean analyzing but rather discovering the pleasure in simply observing and participating in nature.*

Find a small part of God's creation and spend a few minutes enjoying and engaging with it.

---

* Summarized from Richard Foster, *Prayer* (San Francisco: Harper Collins, 1992), 87–90.

HEAT HAZARDS

Heat stroke, or hyperthermia, is the most dangerous stage of heat-related distress on the body.

STAGES OF WORSENING HYPERTHERMIA
- Heat cramps
  - Profuse sweating
  - Extreme fatigue
  - Muscle cramps
- Heat exhaustion (additional symptoms)
  - Headaches
  - Dizziness
  - Nausea and vomiting
- Heat stroke
  - High body temperature reaching 106°F (41.4°C) or higher
  - Absence of sweating
  - Flushed, red skin
  - Rapid pulse
  - Hallucinations
  - Disorientation
  - Coma

COMPLICATIONS OF HEAT STROKE (HYPERTHERMIA)
- Swelling of brain and other vital organs

TREATMENT
- Place the person in the shade or air-conditioning if possible.
- Begin to cool the skin as quickly as possible.
  - Cool water to the skin.
- Place ice packs under the arm pits and in the groin area.
- Continue to cool and monitor body temperature until it reaches 101–102°F (38.5°C).

PREVENTION

- Avoid dehydration.
- Treat the heat cramps and heat exhaustion before it escalates into heat stroke.
- Drink cold, nonalcoholic beverages.
- Replenish electrolytes.
- Wear a hat.
- Wear light-colored, lightweight, loose-fitting clothes.

NOTES

YOU'RE MINE

ISAIAH 43:1-4

1-4 But now, GOD's Message,
the God who made you in the first place, Jacob,
the One who got you started, Israel:
"Don't be afraid, I've redeemed you.
I've called your name. You're mine.
When you're in over your head, I'll be there with you.
When you're in rough waters, you will not go down.
When you're between a rock and a hard place,
it won't be a dead end —
Because I am GOD, your personal God,
The Holy of Israel, your Savior.
I paid a huge price for you:
all of Egypt, with rich Cush and Seba thrown in!
That's how much you mean to me!
That's how much I love you!
I'd sell off the whole world to get you back,
trade the creation just for you."

READ

Read the passage aloud slowly, keeping in mind that God is the speaker.

THINK

Read the passage aloud again even more slowly, pausing between verses. Read it with the idea that God is saying these words directly to you.

1. Of God's words to you in this passage, what is your favorite?
2. Which phrase do you most need to hear from God?

Read the passage one more time. Rest in silence. Wait on God and hear him speaking directly to you.

PRAY

Respond to what God has said to you, perhaps with amazement or gratitude.

LIVE

Read the passage aloud one more time, and hear the echo of the words lingering in the air. Make up a song using a line from these verses. If you wish, use a tune you already know.

ALTITUDE SICKNESS

**AMERICAN RED CROSS DISASTER HEALTH SERVICES
PROTOCOLS**

Acclimatization is the process of the body's adjusting to decreased availability of oxygen at high altitudes. This slow process can take anywhere from a couple of days to weeks.

High altitude is defined as:

- High Altitude: 5,000–11,500 feet
- Very High Altitude: 11,500–18,000 feet
- Extreme Altitude: above 18,000 feet

Altitude sickness rarely occurs below 8,000 feet.
Normal physiologic changes occur with altitude:

- Hyperventilation (breathing faster, deeper, or both)
- Shortness of breath during exertion
- Change of breathing pattern at night
- Increased urination

Being out of breath with exertion is normal, as long as the sensation of shortness of breath subsides quickly with rest.

The change in breathing pattern at night is known as periodic breathing: cycles of normal breathing, which gradually slows, then breath-holding for ten to fifteen seconds, and then recovery or accelerated breathing.

Periodic breathing is not altitude sickness, but usually does not go away without descent.

During acclimatization, the body's chemistry strives to achieve fluid balance, resulting in more frequent urination. If you are not urinating frequently, you may be dehydrated, or you may not be acclimatizing well.

If the body continues to fail to acclimatize at the current altitude, there will be an oxygen debt that will reduce the body's ability to function properly. This is Acute Mountain Sickness (AMS). The symptoms are thought to be due to mild swelling of brain tissue.

If the swelling progresses, brain dysfunction will occur, initiating a condition referred to as High Altitude Cerebral Edema (HACE), in which the brain swells to the point of not being able to function properly. This condition can progress rapidly and be fatal in a matter of a few hours to one or two days.

High Altitude Pulmonary Edema (HAPE) is a severe form of altitude sickness when fluid builds up in the lungs or tissue around the lungs where gas exchange takes place.

SIGNS AND SYMPTOMS
- Acute Mountain Sickness (AMS)
  - Above 8,000 feet.
  - Most common form of altitude sickness.
  - Headache.
  - Loss of appetite, nausea, or vomiting.
  - Fatigue or weakness.
  - Dizziness or light-headed.
  - Difficulty sleeping.
- High Altitude Cerebral Edema (HACE)
  - Change in ability to think.
  - Confusion.
  - Change in behavior, lethargic.
  - Staggering walk or inability to walk a straight line.
  - Because of mental confusion, the patient may not recognize they are sick and in need of help.
- High Altitude Pulmonary Edema (HAPE)
  - Extreme fatigue.
  - Breathlessness at rest.
  - Fast, shallow breathing.
  - Cough with possible frothy or pink sputum.
  - Gurgling or rattling sound in either or both lungs.
  - Tightness of chest, feeling of congestion.
  - Blue or gray lips or fingernails.
  - Drowsiness.
  - Inability to sleep unless sitting up.
  - Usually occurs the second night after an ascent and is more frequent in young climbers or trekkers.
  - Exertion and exposure to cold can raise pulmonary blood

pressure and contribute to the onset or worsening of HAPE.
- Treatment of AMS, HACE, and HAPE
  - Descent: For HACE and HAPE scenarios, immediate descent is prudent. Delay could be fatal.
  - Do not let the person sleep during the critical period of the illness.
  - Administer oxygen if available.
  - Delaying a descent could be fatal.
  - Descend to the last elevation that the person was able to sleep comfortably. If in doubt, descend at least 1,500–3,000 feet if possible.
  - Anticipate having to transport the patient or heavily assist him or her with the descent.
  - HAPE resolves rapidly with descent, and re-ascent is possible after a couple of days of rest.
  - HACE patients usually survive if they descend soon enough and far enough for complete recovery. Re-ascent is acceptable once there are no symptoms, including symptoms of AMS.
  - Avoid caffeinated drinks and alcohol.
  - Headaches are not normal at altitude and could be the first warning sign of AMS. Do not ignore these initial symptoms.

PREVENTION
- Climb gradually.
- Stop for a day or two and rest every 2,000 feet above 8,000 feet.
- Sleep at a lower altitude when possible.
- Early recognition of symptoms.
- While climbing:
  - Drink plenty of fluids.
  - Avoid alcohol.
  - Eat regular meals that are high in carbohydrates.
- Avoid high altitudes if you have heart or lung disease.

FINDING DIRECTION

"I think we are lost" can be tragic words in a wilderness setting. Outdoor activity can sometimes cause us to fail to take note of just how far we have traveled or in what direction we are headed.

Practice these simple tips to help keep you on the right path. Lost people usually travel in circles. Even when we know our walking direction, we are influenced to change our direction without even realizing it. Unseen but real forces are at work, like wind, rain, or an injury or tenderness in a leg or foot. Even sunlight can cause a person wandering or walking to deviate from his or her intended path. When meeting objects in your path, be aware of this tendency and deliberately alternate to the right and to the left when passing obstacles. This will help you to maintain a truer intended line of travel.

It is almost impossible to walk a straight line if you are not using landmarks in front of you and back marks behind you. If natural back marks are lacking, you can make your own to help you stay on track as you move forward and maintain a straight line of travel.

No compass? No map? You can still find direction.

USING THE SUN
Roughly speaking, the sun rises in the east and sets in the west. This is only completely true at the equator. No matter where the compassless natural navigator may be, south can be found when the sun is at its highest point (while in the Northern Hemisphere), or north can be found when the sun is at its highest point (while in the Southern Hemisphere).

USING THE MOON
To find the general direction of north or south at night, observing the moon can help. The moon has no light of its own, but it does reflect the sun. That gives you a heads-up as to direction of the sun. Okay, so what? Well. if the moon is in a crescent phase, simply draw an imaginary line through the tips of its "horns" down to the horizon. Where this point touches is roughly south in the Northern Hemisphere or north in the Southern Hemisphere.

What about finding east and west with the moon? When the moon rises before the sun sets, the illuminated side is facing west. If the moon rises after midnight, the illuminated side is facing east.

USING THE NORTH STAR

This is a basic navigation skill that has been used for thousands of years. The North Star is a valuable navigation tool, because it is located almost directly above the North Pole. It is not a bright star, but it remains in a fixed position through the night, thus offering a constant point of reference.

Knowing how to identify the Big Dipper (Ursa Major) and Cassiopeia (shaped like a W) will be helpful in locating the North Star, because these two constellations never set in the night sky, even though they do not remain in a fixed position. Once you have located the Big Dipper, follow the edge of the cup five times its length toward a medium bright star — that is the North Star. To double-check, find Cassiopeia. The North Star is halfway between Cassiopeia and the Big Dipper.

USING PREVAILING WINDS

If you posses a good sense of observation, prevailing winds can offer clues to direction for the compassless natural navigator. Pay attention to the trees. They are more than just pretty; they are nature's signposts. In areas with strong prevailing winds, this will cause trees to grow and lean in toward a particular direction. Prevailing winds are measured by where the wind is coming from. Trees can have a greater growth of branches and leaves on the sheltered side. Look for these "flag trees" with their branches extended from the pole by the wind.

USING SAND OR SNOW WHEN THERE ARE NO TREES

Wind will pile sand and snow into hills and ridges. Large deposits of sand, like dunes or snowbanks, can indicate the direction of prevailing winds. Do not mistake the direction of dunes and banks with ripples in the sand or snow. Ripples are never very tall, a few inches at the tallest, and can be caused by a sudden wind — not necessarily a prevailing wind. Investigate the prevailing wind direction in the area of your activity.

USING AN ANALOG WATCH (IN THE NORTHERN HEMISPHERE)

Hold your watch horizontally.

- Point the hour hand at the sun.
- The direction midway between the hour and the numeral 12 on your watch will be south on a north-south line.
- If you have doubt as to which end of this midway line is north, remember that the sun rises in the east, sets in the west, and is due south at noon.

JUST A STICK

Get yourself a three-foot stick, and push it into the ground so that it stands upright. Now, mark the tip of the shadow cast by the stick. Wait about fifteen minutes and mark the tip of the second shadow. Now, draw a line through these two marks, and stand with your left foot on the first mark and your right foot on the end of the line you drew through the second mark. You are now facing north if you are in the Northern Hemisphere or south if you are in the Southern Hemisphere.

NOTES

GOD REVEALS HIMSELF

EXODUS 33:21–34:7

21-23 GOD said, "Look, here is a place right beside me. Put yourself on this rock. When my Glory passes by, I'll put you in the cleft of the rock and cover you with my hand until I've passed by. Then I'll take my hand away and you'll see my back. But you won't see my face."

1-3 GOD spoke to Moses: "Cut out two tablets of stone just like the originals and engrave on them the words that were on the original tablets you smashed. Be ready in the morning to climb Mount Sinai and get set to meet me on top of the mountain. Not a soul is to go with you; the whole mountain must be clear of people, even animals — not even sheep or oxen can be grazing in front of the mountain."

4-7 So Moses cut two tablets of stone just like the originals. He got up early in the morning and climbed Mount Sinai as GOD had commanded him, carrying the two tablets of stone. GOD descended in the cloud and took up his position there beside him and called out the name, GOD. GOD passed in front of him and called out, "GOD, GOD, a God of mercy and grace, endlessly patient — so much love, so deeply true — loyal in love for a thousand generations, forgiving iniquity, rebellion, and sin. Still, he doesn't ignore sin. He holds sons and grandsons responsible for a father's sins to the third and even fourth generation."

READ

Read the passage slowly. To get a broader feel for what's happening, quickly read the expanded passage.

THINK

During a second read, explore the nooks and crannies of God's communication with Moses, noticing words that embellish your mental picture of who God is or of the situation at hand. The third time, listen for one or two of God's words that especially impress you. Choose one word or phrase, then take time to repeat it to yourself, letting it interact with your thoughts, feelings, and desires.

PRAY

Deeply ponder the quality of God that the word or phrase portrays. Share with him what's striking to you about this aspect of his character. Explore what makes you desirous of someone with this trait. If more thoughts, feelings, or desires come to the surface, open up to them and ask God to clarify how they expand or even alter your understanding of this part of his personality. End your prayer by letting the word or words drift through your mind and heart again.

LIVE

Envision the ways God is present to you right now. What posture does he have (for example, standing tall, sitting near)? What expression is on his face? If he speaks to you, what tones does his voice hold? Ask him to enhance — and correct, if necessary — in the coming months this picture of how you see him, through the Bible passages you read and through your experiences.

BACKPACKING TIPS

THE BASICS
No matter the length of your trip, consider these ten basics as essential for any backpacking experience:

1. Extra food
2. Extra water
3. Extra clothing (sweater, hat, and raingear)
4. Map of area
5. Compass (with knowledge of how to use it)
6. Flashlight with extra bulb and batteries
7. Pocketknife or multi-tool
8. Fire-making items
9. Basic first aid kit
10. Sun protection (sunglasses, sunscreen, lip balm, and hat)

FOOD AND PROVISIONS
- Stove with all of its parts and accessories
- Full fuel container(s)
- Wide-mouth water bottles (two to three)
- Cooking pot
- Plastic dipping and measuring cup
- Eating and stirring utensil

CLOTHING
- Boots or hiking shoes.
- Sandals for lounging or crossing streams.
- Technical clothing (waterproof, breathable, quick-drying, insulating).
- Waterproof clothing bag or plastic vacuum-pack bag.
- Non-cotton socks.
- Underwear: consider synthetic material that can be easily washed and dries quickly. These also can help guard against chaffing as you hike.

- Pants (non-cotton). Investigate the technical clothing that is available.
- Fleece jacket.
- Long-sleeve and short-sleeve shirt (non-cotton, technical clothing suited for the environment and climate — lightweight and quick drying). Learn to layer.

Adapt these basic lists to accommodate your length of stay, season, and location.

NOTES

CAN'T GET ENOUGH

PSALM 63:1-8

1 God — you're my God!
   I can't get enough of you!
I've worked up such hunger and thirst for God,
   traveling across dry and weary deserts.

2-4 So here I am in the place of worship, eyes open,
   drinking in your strength and glory.
In your generous love I am really living at last!
   My lips brim praises like fountains.
I bless you every time I take a breath;
   My arms wave like banners of praise to you.

5-8 I eat my fill of prime rib and gravy;
   I smack my lips. It's time to shout praises!
If I'm sleepless at midnight,
   I spend the hours in grateful reflection.
Because you've always stood up for me,
   I'm free to run and play.
I hold on to you for dear life,
   and you hold me steady as a post.

READ

Read the passage silently and slowly.

PRAY

Tell God how you honestly respond to this psalm.

Perhaps you don't have this drooling, lip-smacking desire for God. Maybe the idea even embarrasses you. Or maybe you'd like to be this way, but it sounds far too spiritual. Reveal your honest feelings to God.

Perhaps you do have these intense feelings for God. If so, which words in the psalm best describe that?

THINK

Read the passage again.

If one word or phrase describes your present state, say it aloud.

If one word or phrase describes how you would like to be, say it aloud.

LIVE

Consider this quotation from *The Cloud of Unknowing*: "Nourish in your heart a lively longing for God."* Bask in that idea, and try to see yourself doing it.

---

* William Johnston, ed., *The Cloud of Unknowing* (New York: Doubleday, 1973), 47.

FOUR WHEELING TIPS

Getting there is part of the adventure. If you are four wheeling, here are a few tips to help you arrive safely and get the most out of your experience:

- Travel on designated roads or trails.
- Travel in areas opened and approved for four-wheel drive vehicles.
- Travel straight up and down hills for added safety.
- Drive over obstacles with your wheel and not around it. You will clear it and also avoid widening the trail.
- Straddle ruts and gullies even if they are wider than your vehicle.
- Most four-by-fours can be driven in axle-deep water without special concerns for the air intake or system electronics.
- Drive slowly and steadily through water to create a bow wave in front of your bumper, thus reducing the height of the water behind the bumper and engine compartment.
- Fast-moving, shallow streams should be crossed at a slight upstream angle. Then turn downstream when exiting to allow the current to help you out. (Never cross fast-flowing deep streams. Your vehicle could be swept away.)
- Go easy on that gas in the mud and try to keep your wheels from spinning. Lowering tire pressure to twenty pounds may help give you more traction.
- After exiting mud or water, be sure to apply your brakes several times to dry them out and have them ready for the next time you will need them.

ATV SPECIFICS
(See www.atvsafety.org.)

- Clothing
  - Helmet use for driver and passenger.
  - Eye protection.
  - Boots, over-the-ankle with low heels to prevent slipping off footrests.

- Gloves.
- Long pants.
- Long-sleeved shirt or jacket.
- Tires
  - Left side and right side tire pressures should be the same to avoid the vehicle's pulling to one side.
  - Underinflated tires can cause wheel damage when passing over rough terrain.
  - Overinflation may easily damage tires.
- Wheels
  - Make sure axle nuts are tight and secured by cotter pins.
  - Make sure wheel nuts are tightened.
- Brakes
  - Maintained, adjusted according to owner's manual.
- Nuts and Bolts
  - Rough terrain will loosen parts.
  - While engine is off, inspect for loose parts.
  - Shake handlebars and footrests.
  - Check major fasteners.
- Riding Posture
  - Head and eyes up, looking well ahead.
  - Shoulders relaxed with elbows bent slightly, out and away from your body.
  - Knees in toward the gas tank.
  - Feet on the footrests, with toes pointing straight ahead.
  - This initial position will best allow you to quickly react and shift weight as your course may dictate.
- Low to moderate speed turns
  - Move your body weight forward and to the inside of the turn.
  - When riding with a passenger, weight shift should mirror the operator.
  - Turn handlebars while looking in the direction of the turn.
- Increased speeds or sharper turns
  - Move your body weight farther toward the inside of the turn.
  - If tipping begins, lean farther into the turn while gradually reducing the throttle and begin making a wider turn, if possible.
- Hills
  - If you cannot see over the crest of the hill, slow down until you

have a clear view.

- Keep your weight uphill at all times.
- When approaching an uphill climb, keep your feet firmly on the footrests.
- Move up on the seat and lean forward or stand and position your torso over the front wheels.
- Passengers should mirror the operator's weight shift.
- If you do not have enough power to reach the top of a hill but still have forward momentum and enough room to turn around safely:
  - Keep your weight uphill.
  - Make a U-turn and continue downhill in a lower gear.
  - Do not attempt to ride backward down a hill.
  - If you begin rolling backward, do not apply the rear brake abruptly. (Using the rear brake alone or abruptly could cause the ATV to roll over backward.) Keep your weight uphill and apply the front brake.
  - When going downhill:
    - Shift your weight to the rear (uphill).
    - Keep the speed low.
    - Use gradual braking.
    - Use lower gear.
    - Passenger's weight shift should mirror the operator's.
  - Traversing a hill:
    - Keep both feet firmly on the footrests.
    - Lean your upper body uphill.
    - If you are on soft terrain, turn your wheels slightly uphill to keep your ATV on a straight line across the hill.
    - If you begin to tip, turn the front wheels downhill if possible. If not, dismount on the uphill side immediately.
    - Avoid sudden throttle changes.

THE GIFT OF SCRIPTURE

PSALM 119:89-101,105

89-96　What you say goes, GOD,
　　　and *stays*, as permanent as the heavens.
　　Your truth never goes out of fashion;
　　　it's as up-to-date as the earth when the sun comes up.
　　Your Word and truth are dependable as ever;
　　　that's what you ordered — you set the earth going.
　　If your revelation hadn't delighted me so,
　　　I would have given up when the hard times came.
　　But I'll never forget the advice you gave me;
　　　you saved my life with those wise words.
　　Save me! I'm all yours.
　　　I look high and low for your words of wisdom.
　　The wicked lie in ambush to destroy me,
　　　but I'm only concerned with your plans for me.
　　I see the limits to everything human,
　　　but the horizons can't contain your commands!

97-101　Oh, how I love all you've revealed;
　　　I reverently ponder it all the day long.
　　Your commands give me an edge on my enemies;
　　　they never become obsolete.
　　I've even become smarter than my teachers
　　　since I've pondered and absorbed your counsel.
　　I've become wiser than the wise old sages
　　　simply by doing what you tell me.
　　I watch my step, avoiding the ditches and ruts of evil
　　　so I can spend all my time keeping your Word. . . .

105　By your words I can see where I'm going;
　　　they throw a beam of light on my dark path.

READ

Read the passage very slowly. Then read it again, this time even slower.

THINK

You've probably heard people say, "The Lord spoke to me," or "God told me x-y-z," and then been left feeling disbelief, confusion, frustration, or guilt. God does speak to us but not in a booming voice that sounds like actor James Earl Jones. God speaks to us through different means: creation, other people's words of guidance, promptings of the Holy Spirit, and "a gentle and quiet whisper" (1 Kings 19:12). But he also speaks to us through his Message.

Explore your attitudes or preconceived ideas about God's Message. Be brutally honest with yourself and God. Think of ways you could value God's Message more and find yourself more attentive to what it has to say.

Spend several minutes considering how God might be speaking to you through this passage concerning his Message.

PRAY

Pray through this passage of Scripture. Simply make the passage your very own, turning the words back to God (rephrased in your own words, if you wish) as a way to converse with him. Be assured that he is listening to you.

LIVE

Invite God to reveal general and specific elements of Scripture to guide your words, thoughts, and actions today.

RIVER CROSSINGS

SCOUTING

Possible safe crossing characteristics:

- Relatively wide stretch of the river.
- Sections of the river with many braided channels are usually shallow and reduce the water's force on your body.
- Be sure to check out downriver for potential hazards in case of a fall or the need for rescue.

CROSSING

- Unbuckle the hip belt and sternum strap of your backpack.
- If you know you will be crossing water, you should have your pack contents secured in waterproof stuff sacks.
- Your hiking conditions and weather will determine whether or not to cross in your hiking boots or some other footwear, like sandals or even barefoot.
- Consider removing your socks to keep them dry for the other side. (Continued hiking following a river crossing will help your boots to dry out.)
- Increase points of contact with the river bottom, either by using a trekking pole or walking stick or by crossing in a group.
- Crossing in a group:
  - Stand abreast or in line by joining arms or hanging on to each other's backpacks.
  - Place the strongest person or the person with the most experience on the upstream side.
  - Take short steps in unison and talk through each movement.
  - Plan each step prior to moving.
  - Use trekking poles to explore the next foot plant.
  - If the river bottom becomes soft or rocks seem to fall away under your footing, retrace your steps and change your course. This could be the edge of a deep hole.

FINAL THOUGHT

If you are in doubt about the crossing, DON'T. This could save your life.

NOTES

_____

_____

_____

_____

_____

_____

_____

_____

_____

_____

_____

_____

_____

_____

_____

_____

_____

_____

_____

_____

_____

_____

_____

_____

COURAGEOUS WHEN IT COUNTS

JOSHUA 1:1-9

1-9   After the death of Moses the servant of GOD, GOD spoke to Joshua, Moses' assistant:

"Moses my servant is dead. Get going. Cross this Jordan River, you and all the people. Cross to the country I'm giving to the People of Israel. I'm giving you every square inch of the land you set your foot on — just as I promised Moses. From the wilderness and this Lebanon east to the Great River, the Euphrates River — all the Hittite country — and then west to the Great Sea. It's all yours. All your life, no one will be able to hold out against you. In the same way I was with Moses, I'll be with you. I won't give up on you; I won't leave you. Strength! Courage! You are going to lead this people to inherit the land that I promised to give their ancestors. Give it everything you have, heart and soul. Make sure you carry out The Revelation that Moses commanded you, every bit of it. Don't get off track, either left or right, so as to make sure you get to where you're going. And don't for a minute let this Book of The Revelation be out of mind. Ponder and meditate on it day and night, making sure you practice everything written in it. Then you'll get where you're going; then you'll succeed. Haven't I commanded you? Strength! Courage! Don't be timid; don't get discouraged. GOD, your God, is with you every step you take."

READ

As you read the passage, imagine that you wrote these words yourself and are now reflecting on what you wrote.

THINK

Israel is grieving the loss of its trusted leader, Moses. But with every ending comes a new beginning. In the midst of the mourning, God approaches Joshua and assures him that he is the man to lead the people into the Promised Land. God promises Joshua that he will be with him and that the land will be given to the nation of Israel. God commands Joshua to be courageous and tells him to remain committed to the study of his Word.

Read verse 9 again. Is embracing these words in your life hard or easy? At what times are you scared? Why? When you are fearful, what can you do about it?

PRAY

Be blatantly honest with God about your fears, worries, concerns, and anxieties. Tell him exactly why you are scared, and be assured that he hears you. Thank him for listening. Then reread the passage, personalizing the words by making God's words to Joshua your very own.

LIVE

When you find yourself in situations that expose your fears, remember the promises of God—his presence and his guidance for you into the future.

SAFETY ON ICE

Montana State Government Fish, Wildlife, and Parks Information, Minnesota Department of Natural Resources, and New Hampshire Fish and Game Department, among other government agencies, offer the following guidelines and recommendations when venturing out onto the ice.

GENERAL CHARACTERISTICS
- Blue ice is usually hard.
- Opaque, gray, dark, or porous spots in the ice indicate weak, soft areas.
- Ice thins more quickly along the shorelines.
- Pressure ridges (where ice has cracked and heaved due to expansion from freezing) can indicate thin ice.
- Dark snow layer on top of the ice can indicate unsafe ice.
- Avoid areas with currents and bridges.

THICKNESS GUIDELINES FOR NEW, CLEAR ICE ONLY
- Two inches or less: STAY OFF.
- Four inches: ice fishing or other activities on foot.
- Five inches: snowmobile or ATV.
- Eight to twelve inches: car or small pickup.
- Twelve to fifteen inches: medium truck.
- Check the ice thickness in several places.

SAFETY PRACTICES ON THE ICE
- Dress in layers. Wool, silk, and some synthetics will keep you warm, even when wet.
- Wear insulated waterproof boots, gloves, and a windbreaker.
- Go with a partner and maintain a safe distance between each other while moving on the ice, in case one of you falls through the ice.
- Attach a pair of long spikes or commercial ice-fishing picks on a heavy string and carry them around your neck. If you break

through the ice, you can use the spikes to assist in pulling yourself out of the water.

- Wear ice cleats to avoid falls.
- Carry a rope to throw to someone who falls through the ice.

IF YOU BREAK THROUGH THE ICE

- Turn toward the direction you came from. This is probably the strongest ice.
- Place your hands and arms on the unbroken surface. If you have spikes or ice picks, use them to as you attempt to pull yourself out.
- To aid with pulling yourself out kick your feet as if swimming while pulling with your arms. This will help to lift your body onto the ice.
- Lie flat on the ice and roll to safety. Do not stand up close to the broken ice.

IF SOMEONE ELSE BREAKS THROUGH THE ICE

- Reach them from shore, if possible. Extend an object like a rope, ladder, or even jumper cables. If the fallen person begins to pull you in, release your grip and start over.
  - If on the ice with him, lie down flat and reach with some object or form a human chain. Do not stand near him on the ice while attempting a rescue.
  - After securing the person, wiggle backward to solid ice.
  - Get the person sheltered, warm, and dry immediately.
- Toss: If he cannot be reached, then toss him one end of a rope or something that will float. Have the victim tie the rope around himself immediately in case he loses the ability to do so later because of the cold and effects of hypothermia.
- Row: If a light boat is available, push it across the ice ahead of you and to the edge of the hole. Get into the boat and pull the victim in over the bow.
- Go: If the situation is too dangerous for you to perform the rescue, call 911 or get help.

FOUR STAGES OF IMMERSION IN COLD WATER

- Stage 1: Cold Water Shock
  - This response begins immediately upon immersion and will peak in the first thirty seconds to five minutes.

- Breathing changes are immediate and may include involuntary gasping, rapid breathing, dizziness, and confusion.
- Wearing a life jacket prior to a fall will greatly reduce the chances of water aspiration.
- Stage 2: Swim Failure
  - After three to thirty minutes, it becomes increasingly more difficult to swim or move.
  - Nerves and muscles in the arms and legs cool quickly due to blood diverted away from extremities in an attempt to keep the core and vital organs warm.
  - Manual dexterity, grip strength, and movement speed will drop 60 to 80 percent.
- Stage 3: Hypothermia
  - Someone who survives the first two stages of cold-water immersion will face the onset of hypothermia.
  - The continuous loss of body heat and resulting decrease in core body temperature can result in death.
- Stage 4: Post-Rescue Collapse
  - A person is still at risk after having been rescued from the cold-water immersion.
  - During the process of hypothermia, the vascular system and its ability to move blood is impaired.
  - The body will try to rewarm itself, and this can put a huge load on the heart.

If you plan to be on the ice, consider assembling and always carrying your own ice safety kit. This kit could include an ice pick or sharpened screwdrivers carried around your neck, rope, and a whistle to call for help.

NOTES

TRUSTING AND EXPECTANT

JOHN 3:9-11,14-15,17-21

9-11   Nicodemus asked, "What do you mean by this? How does this happen?"

Jesus said, "You're a respected teacher of Israel and you don't know these basics? Listen carefully. I'm speaking sober truth to you. I speak only of what I know by experience; I give witness only to what I have seen with my own eyes. There is nothing secondhand here, no hearsay. Yet instead of facing the evidence and accepting it, you procrastinate with questions." . . .

14-15   "In the same way that Moses lifted the serpent in the desert so people could have something to see and then believe, it is necessary for the Son of Man to be lifted up — and everyone who looks up to him, trusting and expectant, will gain a real life, eternal life. . . .

17-18   "God didn't go to all the trouble of sending his Son merely to point an accusing finger, telling the world how bad it was. He came to help, to put the world right again. Anyone who trusts in him is acquitted; anyone who refuses to trust him has long since been under the death sentence without knowing it. And why? Because of that person's failure to believe in the one-of-a-kind Son of God when introduced to him.

19-21   "This is the crisis we're in: God-light streamed into the world, but men and women everywhere ran for the darkness. They went for the darkness because they were not really interested in pleasing God. Everyone who makes a practice of doing evil, addicted to denial and illusion, hates God-light and won't come near it, fearing a painful exposure. But anyone working and living in truth and reality welcomes God-light so the work can be seen for the God-work it is."

READ

Before you read the passage, understand that Jesus has just told Nicodemus (a scholar and teacher) that he must be "'born from above' by the wind of God, the Spirit of God" (verse 8). But Nicodemus is confused! Now read the passage silently.

THINK

Read the passage again, aloud this time, putting yourself in the place of Nicodemus standing on the rooftop in the moonlight, receiving Jesus' words.

1. Which words or phrases stand out to you? Consider these:

   □ "Everyone who looks up to him, trusting and expectant, will gain a real life, eternal life."
   □ "God didn't go to all the trouble of sending his Son merely to point an accusing finger, . . . [the Son] came to help, to put the world right again."
   □ "Anyone who trusts in him is acquitted."
   □ "God-light streamed into the world."
   □ "Anyone working and living in truth and reality welcomes God-light so the work can be seen for the God-work it is."

2. Why?

PRAY

Talk to Jesus about any phrases that confused you. Talk to him about the phrases that captivated you.

LIVE

Sit quietly before God. Put yourself in the place of Nicodemus again — possibly lying in your bed each night, going over these words Jesus said to you. Which words will you drift off with tonight?

DESERT TIPS

Contact your local Forestry Service, Bureau of Land Management, or Game and Fish Divisions for information on possible water sources, such as holes, wells, tanks, and guzzlers (used by conservation services to water both small and large game animals).

WHAT TO PACK (NOT INTENDED FOR WINTER EXPERIENCE)

- Outerwear
  - Waterproof, breathable jacket
  - Fleece jacket or wool sweater
  - Convertible hiking pants
- Base Layer
  - Midweight long john top
  - Midweight long john bottoms
  - Synthetic briefs or bra
  - Synthetic T-shirt
  - Cotton T-shirt
- Accessories
  - Wool or fleece hat
  - Leather gloves
- Footwear
  - Trail shoe or hiking boot, depending on the length of trip
  - Liner socks (two)
  - Wool or synthetic socks (three)
  - Camp footwear
- Extras
  - Sun hat
  - Bandanna
  - Personal locator beacon, like SPOT personal GPS locator
- Gear
  - Backpack
  - Screen tent or tarp
  - Three-season sleeping bag (even in the summer, night temperatures can drop to near freezing)

- Sleeping pad
- Trekking poles
- Canister stove and fuel canisters
- Fire-making kit
- Cook set
  - Eating utensils
  - Bowl or Sierra cup
- Headlamp with extra bulb and batteries
- 32-ounce water bottles (at least two)
- Water treatment (filter, tablets, or drops)
- Pocketknife or multi-tool
- Area map, compass, and/or GPS
- Sunglasses
- Trip-appropriate first aid kit (Be sure to include tweezers for cactus spine removal.)
- Ziplock bags
- Insect repellant
- Sunscreen
- Lip balm
- Toilet paper and trowel (The National Park Service requires you to bury feces at least six inches and pack toilet paper back out, thus the ziplock bags.)

WATER CONSIDERATIONS

- It is generally recommended to drink at least one gallon of water each day in the desert.
- Never pass a water source without drinking as much as possible and filling your water bottles.
- Store on the trail as you go in, to be used on your return.
- Store water in your vehicle for your return.
- Your body can only absorb about a quart of fluid per hour.
  - Do not wait until you are thirsty to drink.
  - Drink small amounts often.

LEARNING TO PAY ATTENTION

EXODUS 3:1-6

1-2 Moses was shepherding the flock of Jethro, his father-in-law, the priest of Midian. He led the flock to the west end of the wilderness and came to the mountain of God, Horeb. The angel of GOD appeared to him in flames of fire blazing out of the middle of a bush. He looked. The bush was blazing away but it didn't burn up.

3 Moses said, "What's going on here? I can't believe this! Amazing! Why doesn't the bush burn up?"

4 GOD saw that he had stopped to look. God called to him from out of the bush, "Moses! Moses!"

He said, "Yes? I'm right here!"

5 God said, "Don't come any closer. Remove your sandals from your feet. You're standing on holy ground."

6 Then he said, "I am the God of your father: The God of Abraham, the God of Isaac, the God of Jacob."

Moses hid his face, afraid to look at God.

READ

Read the passage aloud.

THINK

Moses is shepherding his father-in-law's sheep. In the distance he sees a bush in flames, but the bush mysteriously doesn't burn up. He walks closer, perhaps expecting a miracle, only to have a more unique encounter than he ever imagined. He interacts with the living God.

When have you experienced a unique encounter with the living God? What was your burning bush like?

What do you think God meant when he said, "Remove your sandals from your feet. You're standing on holy ground"?

God is holy. What difference does that make in your life?

PRAY

Ask God to reveal himself to you today in a fresh way, a way that he has never revealed himself before.

LIVE

Moses heard from God when he paid attention. Like Moses, we often encounter God when we pay attention to what's going on around us. Find a quiet place and spend a few moments in utter silence, paying attention to those aspects of your life that you often neglect: people, situations, quiet moments, creation, and so on. As you do this, look for God waiting there to interact with you.

SURVIVAL AT SEA OR IN OPEN WATER

WATER SURVIVAL TIPS
- Whenever possible, make your way to a raft or floating debris.
- Relax; your body will be more buoyant when it is relaxed.
- Floating on your back requires the least amount of energy.
  - Lie on your back in the water.
  - Spread your arms and legs.
  - Arch your back.
  - Control your breathing. This will maintain your face out of the water.
- If waves are too big or if the water is too rough to float on your back, then float facedown.
- Best swimming strokes in a survival situation:
  - Dog paddle: Excellent stroke with clothing or wearing a life jacket. Requires little energy. Slow.
  - Breaststroke: Use to swim underwater, through oil or debris, or in rough seas. Best stroke for long-range swimming.
  - Sidestroke: A good relief stroke.
  - Backstroke: Another excellent relief stroke.
- Floating with only a life preserver: assume the HELP body position:
  - Heat Escaping Lessening Position (HELP).
  - Remain still and assume fetal position to help retain body heat.
  - The majority loss of body heat is through your head. Keep it out of the water.

COLD WEATHER CONSIDERATIONS
- Put on any extra clothing available. Keep clothes loose.
- Rig windbreak, spray shield, or canopy in raft.
- Try to maintain floor of raft dry, and cover if possible to add some insulation from the cold.
- Huddle with others to keep warm. Move occasionally to aid in

good blood circulation. Cover the group if possible.

- If food is available, give extra rations to those suffering with hypothermia.
- Heat exchange in water is twenty-five times greater than it is in air.

HOT WEATHER CONDITIONS

- Rig a sunshade or canopy, but allow for ventilation.
- Cover your skin to protect from sunburn.
- Protect your eyelids, the back of your ears, and the skin under your chin.
- Use sunglasses with UV protection, or improvise eye protection.
- Use sparingly the practice of moistening clothing to keep you cool if you are in saltwater. The overuse could lead to boils, sores, and other skin irritations due to the salt content and could cause added health concerns.

RATIONING WATER

After exposure, your primary survival need is water.

- Keep your body well-shaded to minimize perspiration.
- Do not exert yourself.
- Sleep when possible.
- If you do not have water, do not eat.
- If you can ration 2 liters (2.1 quarts) of water, then eat.
- If nauseated and vomiting, rest and relax. Vomiting loses great amounts of water.
- Watch for clouds and be ready for any chance of rain.
- At night, secure a tarp (if available) and turn the edges up to collect the dew.
- Dew also can form on the side of the raft. Use a sponge or cloth to collect it.
- When it rains, drink as much as you can hold.
- Water from fresh fish:
  - Drink the fluid found along the spine, and suck the fluid from the eyes of large fish.
  - If you are short on water and need to do this, do not drink any other body fluids from the fish. They will be rich in protein and fat and will require more water to digest than they will supply.

POSSIBLE HEALTH CONCERNS

- Seasickness — nausea and vomiting caused by the motion can lead to:
  - Extreme fluid loss and exhaustion.
  - Loss of will to survive.
  - Others becoming sick.
  - Attraction of sharks.
  - Unclean conditions from vomiting can promote further health complications.
  - What to do?
    - Wash the patient and raft as best as possible, removing the sight and odor of the vomit.
    - Keep the patient from eating while nausea persists.
    - Keep the patient lying down and resting.
- Sores
  - Skin exposed to water, especially saltwater for extended periods of time, can develop sores.
  - If the sores form scabs or fill with pus, do not open or drain them. Flush with fresh water, if possible, and allow them to dry.
- Difficulty Urinating
  - Most likely due to dehydration.
  - Leave it alone, as it could lead to further dehydration.

DETECTING LAND

- Fixed cumulus clouds in a clear sky while other clouds are moving can indicate land mass.
- Greenish tint in the sky could be reflection of sunlight off shallow lagoons or coral reefs.
- Light-colored reflections on clouds can indicate ice fields or snow-covered land. These reflections will be distinctly different from reflection caused by the open water.
- Shallow water will have a lighter color than deep water.
- At night, or when there is fog, mist, or rain, odors and sounds from land may be easily detected. Listen for the roar of the surf. You will hear the breaking waves before you see the surf.
- Cries of seabirds from one direction indicate a roosting area.
- The direction of birds' flight at dawn and at dusk may indicate the direction of land.

- During the day, birds are looking for food, and direction of flight will not be helpful.
- Mirages can occur over water too, so be careful. Try looking at it from a different angle. Mirages will disappear when viewed from another angle.

NOTES

GOD SHOWS UP

ZEPHANIAH 2:3,6-10

3   Seek GOD, all you quietly disciplined people
        who live by GOD's justice.
    Seek GOD's right ways. Seek a quiet and disciplined life.
        Perhaps you'll be hidden on the Day of GOD's anger. . . .

6-7   The lands of the seafarers
        will become pastureland,
    A country for shepherds and sheep.
        What's left of the family of Judah will get it.
    Day after day they'll pasture by the sea,
        and go home in the evening to Ashkelon to sleep.
    Their very own GOD will look out for them.
        He'll make things as good as before.

8-10   "I've heard the crude taunts of Moab,
        the mockeries flung by Ammon,
    The cruel talk they've used to put down my people,
        their self-important strutting along Israel's borders.
    Therefore, as sure as I am the living God," says
        GOD-of-the-Angel-Armies,
        Israel's personal God,
    "Moab will become a ruin like Sodom,
        Ammon a ghost town like Gomorrah,
    One a field of rocks, the other a sterile salt flat,
        a moonscape forever.
    What's left of my people will finish them off,
        will pick them clean and take over.
    This is what they get for their bloated pride,
        Their taunts and mockeries of the people
        of GOD-of-the-Angel-Armies."

READ

Read the passage aloud slowly and silently.

You've probably experienced the wrath of a bully. The nation of Moab had been bullying the nation of Judah. In this passage God says that he plans to sweep in and save Judah. The encouraging words in verses 6-7 are spoken of Judah; verses 8-10 are indictments of Moab to defend Judah.

THINK

Read the passage again, noting the primary sins of Moab. As you read, grieve over them:

- cruelty, mockery, and taunts
- put-downs, self-importance, and pride

In what ways do these two sets of sins feed off each other?

When have you experienced such treatment? In what way did God intervene to rescue you? If you don't feel that God did so, take this rescue of Judah and appropriate it for yourself. This isn't fantasy — God did rescue you in some way, even if you didn't realize it.

PRAY

Thank God for rescuing you and providing moments of pastureland in your life. Ask God if he wants to use you to rescue someone. Listen for his guidance in doing so.

LIVE

Sit quietly before God. Feel in your gut the sensation of humiliation at someone else's self-importance. Then feel in your gut the sensations of safety and rescue. Understand that you are reliving Judah's experience.

FOREST FIRE

Wildfires can travel quickly and even jump roads, streams, and other bare areas. An attempt to outrun a blaze may prove impossible. Here are some other things to consider if you are faced with this emergency.

- Best escape routes will be roads or a stream that can be quickly traveled with fewer obstacles.
- Forest fires travel faster uphill. Moving downhill may be the better option.
- If you are trapped, move to the middle of an area with the least burnable vegetation. Or, if time permits, burn your own safe zone and lie in the middle after the vegetation has burned off.
- Lakes, ponds, plowed fields, and bare, rocky terrain offer the best protection.
- Evergreen trees burn more quickly than deciduous trees. Escape through a stand of deciduous trees rather than pine trees if possible.
- Avoid areas with dry, dead vegetation.
- If no other shelter is available, find or dig a ditch and lie as flat as possible with your face down in the dirt.
- When the fire has passed, proceed upwind where the fire has already moved through.
- Note that synthetic clothing (including underwear) can melt, adding another element of concern.
- Use leather gloves if you have them to protect your hands as you protect your head or neck while lying flat.
- Avoid narrow draws, chutes, and chimneys when in the mountains as smoke, flames, and hot gases are funneled through these natural channels.
- Avoid ridges and saddles between peaks as they also draw smoke, flames, and gases.
- Protect your air passage and lungs at all costs.
- Personal fire shelters weighing about five pounds can be purchased.

SURVIVING A BEAR ATTACK

Know what to do, should your outdoor adventure bring you into close proximity with a defensive or predatory bear.

GRIZZLY
- Usually medium to dark brown fur
- Distinct shoulder hump (muscle mass that aids the bear in digging roots and slashing prey)
- Average height of 6.5 feet
- Long claws
- Mostly found in Canada, Alaska, Washington, Idaho, the Dakotas, and Montana

BLACK BEAR
- Variety of colors, ranging from black to light blond
- Absence of shoulder hump that Grizzlies possess
- Smaller than Grizzlies with shorter claws
- Most common in North America
- Can be found in all of the provinces of Canada and forty-one of the fifty states in the U.S.

ENCOUNTERING A BEAR

American natives to Alaska and the Yukon Territory believed that bears were just another species of man and understood that they could be extremely dangerous. When coming up on a bear, it is told they would place their hands high above their heads, greet their brother bear, offer an apology for disturbing him, and then quietly retreat.

This is actually a good practice and Plan A when traveling in known bear country. Move forward while talking, singing, or making some other noise in order to alert the bear. Typically they will avoid confrontation. The most likely exception would be the polar bear, which has been known to stalk and hunt man for food. If this tactic of apology and making yourself look bigger than you really are works, well done; but if not, then do not run. The bear most likely will chase you.

Know Plan B if the bear does not share your perception of being brothers. Carry bear pepper/deterrent spray. Do not run. Bears can run up to thirty miles per hour. Drop to the ground in a fetal position, covering the back of your neck with your hands and using your pack to guard your back. Play dead. The bear may stop attacking if it feels you are no longer a threat. Continue to play dead if the bear decides to leave.

If you choose to engage and fight back, straight line front kicks to the head or gut while moving uphill, keeping the bear on the downhill side, will offer you a better defensive strike position.

To help avoid that first potentially dangerous encounter, be sure to put your food, trash, cooking gear, soaps, and toiletries up a bear pole or tree at least twelve feet off the ground. Then place your camp a safe distance from your bear bag.

NOTES

NOTHING BETWEEN US AND GOD'S LOVE

ROMANS 8:31-39

31-39 So, what do you think? With God on our side like this, how can we lose? If God didn't hesitate to put everything on the line for us, embracing our condition and exposing himself to the worst by sending his own Son, is there anything else he wouldn't gladly and freely do for us? And who would dare tangle with God by messing with one of God's chosen? Who would dare even to point a finger? The One who died for us — who was raised to life for us! — is in the presence of God at this very moment sticking up for us. Do you think anyone is going to be able to drive a wedge between us and Christ's love for us? There is no way! Not trouble, not hard times, not hatred, not hunger, not homelessness, not bullying threats, not backstabbing, not even the worst sins listed in Scripture:

> They kill us in cold blood because they hate you.
> We're sitting ducks; they pick us off one by one.

None of this fazes us because Jesus loves us. I'm absolutely convinced that nothing — nothing living or dead, angelic or demonic, today or tomorrow, high or low, thinkable or unthinkable — absolutely *nothing* can get between us and God's love because of the way that Jesus our Master has embraced us.

READ

Read the passage four times very slowly.

THINK

Logically understanding that God loves us is fairly easy. But grasping this truth to its fullest extent in our hearts and souls — in every corner of our everyday existence — requires more. We think we know God loves us, but we don't often ponder this profound truth, this important element of our identity as God's children.

Read the passage again. This time underline the phrases that speak directly to you and encourage your heart. With each underline, say aloud, "Thank you, God, for how much you love me."

"Do you think anyone is going to be able to drive a wedge between [you] and Christ's love for [you]? . . . No way!" When you read Paul's words, what flows through your mind and heart?

PRAY

Sit in silence with one thought in mind: *I am loved by God.* If your mind begins to wander, simply whisper, "Thank you for loving me, Jesus." Claim the promises of this passage as your own.

LIVE

Live confidently knowing that "absolutely *nothing* can get between [you] and God's love." He loves you that much!

CHOOSING THE RIGHT CAMO

BASIC GUIDELINES
- Use a camouflage pattern that is appropriate for your hunting location.
- Full camo is the most effective camo. Include hands, face, and neck areas.
- Cover anything that can reflect or that can be noisy. Include watches, buttons, zippers, and snaps.
- Buy your pants longer than normal to cover your socks or boots when kneeling or sitting.
- Boots should have a dark sole. Be careful of bright logos on the bottom of the boot.
- Set up in the shadows rather than in direct sunlight. In the morning, face west if possible. In the afternoon, face east. If you are in open country, try to keep the sun at your back.
- Avoid setting up at eye level with the animal you are hunting. Remain low on the ground or above in a tree stand.
- Scent elimination should be combined with the correct camouflage.

CHOOSING THE RIGHT CAMOUFLAGE PATTERN
- Mossy Oak Tree Stand
  - Designed for hunting from an elevated position.
  - Design alters the hunter's silhouette among bare tree limbs in late fall.
  - Incorporated tree limbs in the pattern.
  - Digital technology reproduced details of actual tree limbs laid over neutral tones most commonly seen when looking up through bare trees.
  - Ideal for whitetail deer hunters.

- Mossy Oak Duck Blind
    - Designed for marshes, potholes, riverbanks, reeds, tules, bottomland, as well as corn, wheat, and rice fields.
    - The design includes elements from every sector of North America's main waterfowl highway.
    - Base background of true dirt colors, with different tones to represent wet and dry ground.
    - Elements of millet, wild oats, corn stalks, phragmites, Johnson grass, soybeans, and native grasses.
    - Unique shadows enhance depth and create a 3-D effect.
    - Muted shades of brown, tan, gray, and soft black allow blending into harvested fields, marshes, and wetlands.
    - Ideal for duck and goose hunters.
- Mossy Oak Brush
    - Designed for open-range hunting where there is little to no cover available.
    - Background consists of dead grasses and dirt elements.
    - Base coloration blends virtually into any open country surrounding.
    - Varying sizes and shades of authentic brush and other native plants.
    - Soft, naturally occurring shadow patterns.
    - Ideal for the western big game hunter.
- Mossy Oak Break-Up
    - Realistic bark background.
    - Soft, grey oak limbs.
    - Deep shadows to enhance the 3-D illusion.
    - Natural contrast found in the woods is achieved through the details of the pattern.
    - Includes digitized elements of bark, branches, and leaves.
    - Ideal for deer hunting in the cold months of the year.
- Mossy Oak Obsession
    - Digitized lighter background with variety of woodland and non-woodland elements.
    - Realistic limb and ghost shadows.
    - Spring-tone elements.
    - Addition of more green elements.
    - Ideal for a variety of geographic locations and season to season.

- Mossy Oak Break-Up Infinity
  - Features unprecedented depth, unequaled detail, and elements with remarkable contrast.
  - Contains specific elements of leaves, limbs, acorns, and branches that have been selected to create an unmatched realism and contrast to break up a hunter's silhouette.
  - The elements are placed over multiple layers of actual images from the woods to create a multi-dimensional depth of field.
- Mossy Oak Bottomland
  - The original Mossy Oak pattern designed by Toxey Haas in 1986.
  - Used as the foundation for all later patterns.
  - Designed using bark and moss from an oak tree in South Alabama.
  - Colored with dull, flat colors from real dirt, leaves, bark, and old moss in order to blend in with the ground and understory of hardwoods and swampy areas.
  - The New Bottomland pattern preserves the original while applying advanced technology for increased stealth and effectiveness.
  - Allows the hunter to blend into dark environments and obscure his outline from every angle.

NOTES

LIFTING THE VEIL

2 CORINTHIANS 3:12-18

12-15 With that kind of hope to excite us, nothing holds us back. Unlike Moses, we have nothing to hide. Everything is out in the open with us. He wore a veil so the children of Israel wouldn't notice that the glory was fading away — and they *didn't* notice. They didn't notice it then and they don't notice it now, don't notice that there's nothing left behind that veil. Even today when the proclamations of that old, bankrupt government are read out, they can't see through it. Only Christ can get rid of the veil so they can see for themselves that there's nothing there.

16-18 Whenever, though, they turn to face God as Moses did, God removes the veil and there they are — face-to-face! They suddenly recognize that God is a living, personal presence, not a piece of chiseled stone. And when God is personally present, a living Spirit, that old, constricting legislation is recognized as obsolete. We're free of it! All of us! Nothing between us and God, our faces shining with the brightness of his face. And so we are transfigured much like the Messiah, our lives gradually becoming brighter and more beautiful as God enters our lives and we become like him.

READ

Read the passage aloud slowly.

THINK

Again, slowly read verses 12-15 with a mood of despair. Then read verses 16-18 with a mood of joy, mystery, and surprise.

1. What words or phrases stand out to you? Why?
2. If you didn't choose words or phrases from verses 16-18, do that now. Read them again and note the frequency of these words: *face, personal, personally, bright, brighter, brightness.*

PRAY

Paraphrase verses 16-18 back to God, something like: Whenever I turn my face to you, O God, you remove the veil and there we are — face-to-face! I will suddenly recognize you as a living, personal presence, not [fill in, perhaps: a remote, unknown figure]. And when you are personally present, a living Spirit, that old, constricting legalism is recognized as obsolete. I'm free of it! All of us are! Nothing between me and you, my face shining with the brightness of your face. And so I am transfigured much like the Messiah. My life gradually becomes brighter and more beautiful as you enter my life and I become like you.

LIVE

Sit quietly before God, basking in one of these phrases:

- you are "a living, personal presence"
- nothing between you and me
- as you enter my life, it gradually becomes brighter and more beautiful

TREE STAND SAFETY GUIDELINES

Consider these tree stand safety practices as promoted by the Treestand Manufacturer's Association (TMA) at www.tmastands.com.

- Always wear a Fall-Arrest System (FAS)/full body harness that meets TMA standards, even during ascent and descent. Be aware that single strap belts and chest harnesses are no longer considered fall-arrest devices and should not be used. Failure to use an FAS could result in serious injury or death.
- Always read and understand the manufacturer's warnings and instructions before using the tree stand each season. Practice with the tree stand at ground level prior to using at elevated positions. Maintain the warnings and instructions for later review as needed, for instructions on usage for anyone borrowing your stand, or to pass on when selling the tree stand. Use all safety devices provided with your tree stand.
- Never exceed the weight limit specified by the manufacturer.
- Always inspect the tree stand and FAS for signs of wear or damage before each use. The FAS should be discarded or replaced after a fall has occurred.
- Always practice in your full body harness in the presence of a responsible adult prior to using it in an elevated hunting environment, learning what it feels like to hang suspended in it at ground level and how to properly use your suspension relief device.
- Always hunt with a plan and, if possible, a buddy. Before you leave home, let others know your exact hunting location, when you plan to return, and who is with you.
- Always carry emergency signal devices such as a cell phone, walkie-talkie, whistle, signal flare, personal locator device (PLD), and flashlight on your person at all times and within reach, even while you are suspended in your FAS. Watch for changing weather conditions.

- Always select the proper tree for use with your tree stand. Select a live, straight tree that fits within the size limits recommended in your tree stand's instructions. Do not climb or place a tree stand against a leaning tree. Never leave a tree stand installed for more than two weeks, since damage could result from changing weather conditions and/or from other factors not obvious with a visual inspection.
- Always use a haul line to pull up your gear and unloaded firearm or bow to your tree stand once you have reached your desired hunting height. Never climb with anything in your hands or on your back. Prior to descending, lower your equipment on the opposite side of the tree.
- Always know your physical limitations. Don't take chances. Do not climb when using drugs, alcohol, or if you are sick or feeling dizzy.
- Never hurry. While climbing with a tree stand, make slow, even movements of no more than ten to twelve inches at a time. Make sure you have proper contact with the tree and/or tree stand every time you move. On ladder-type tree stands, maintain three points of contact with each step.

NOTES

MAKING THE SHOT: SHOOTING TIPS

The U.S. Marine Corp Marksmanship Center for Excellence identifies five major factors that can affect a shooter hitting the target:

1. Shooter's mental state
2. Windage
3. Lighting
4. Temperature
5. Precipitation

Learn to identify and relate these elements to your shooting situation for better accuracy. Your mental preparedness will be positively affected as you learn to manage the other four factors.

WIND

- Its effect on a round as it travels down range is called deflection.
- Wind deflects the bullet laterally.
- This effect increases with distance to the target.
    - The greater the wind velocity the greater the deflection.
    - Round velocity decreases with distance while wind deflection increases.
- Manage the effects of wind:
    - Identify wind direction. Use flag movement, vegetation movement or feeling the wind against the body.
    - Determine wind value.
        - Full value wind: wind blowing from either the right or left directly across the shooter's front (from 3 o'clock or 9 o'clock). This has the greatest effect on bullet deflection.
        - No value wind: wind blowing directly in the shooter's face (12 o'clock) or his back (6 o'clock). Has no deflection on the bullet.
        - Half value wind: winds blowing from other directions are assigned intermediate values.

- Determining wind velocity:
  - Under 3 mph: barely felt on the face but may be detected by drifting smoke
  - 3–5 mph: felt lightly on the face
  - 5–8 mph: keeps tree leaves in constant motion
  - 8–12 mph: raises dust, dry leaves, or loose paper
  - 12–15 mph: causes small trees to sway
  - 20–25 mph: causes large trees to sway

Using wind direction, value, and velocity, proper sight adjustments can be made. But there are still other factors to be considered.

LIGHTING
- Bright light (clear, blue sky, no haze or fog to filter sunlight).
  - Can make a target appear smaller and farther away.
  - Typically a shooter will overestimate the range.
- Haze (smog, fog, dust, smoke, or humidity).
  - Can make a target appear indistinct.
  - Concentrate on center mass for best results.
- Overcast (solid layer of clouds that block the sun).
  - Makes target appear larger and closer.
  - Typically a shooter will underestimate the range.
- Light overcast: comfortable on the eye, no shine. Perhaps the best lighting condition for shooting.
- Dark, heavy overcast: difficult to identify the target from surroundings.

TEMPERATURE
- Extreme heat:
  - Can lead to rapid fatigue and cause distractions.
  - Can cause blurred vision, muscle cramps, heat exhaustion, and heat stroke.
  - Increase fluid intake, good physical conditioning, and rest breaks will help to offset this effect.
  - High temperatures can produce ground mirages and cause a target to be indistinct or appear to drift from side to side. Maintain center mass hold for the best chance of accuracy.
  - Hot air is less dense than cooler air and has less resistance on the bullet. This allows the bullet to travel faster with less

deflection when wind is present. The tendency would be to aim too high.

- Extreme cold:
  - Can cause the shooter to shiver, be uncomfortable, or experience lapses of memory, all of which can also affect the shooter's mental state.
  - Holding a rifle and trigger-control are difficult with numb fingers.
  - Proper dress is a must in cold climates if you expect to shoot accurately.
  - Extreme cold will cause the bullet to exit the muzzle at a lower velocity and impact the target below the point of aim.
  - Cold air is denser, causing the bullet to experience greater deflection when there is wind.

PRECIPITATION

- Can affect the concentration and comfort of the shooter.
- A positive mental attitude provides the best performance under these conditions.
- Keep moisture out of the bore.

NOTES

SHOT SHELL SELECTION

LEAD SHOT
- Shot size 12, 9, 8 ½: target, practice
- Shot size 8, 7 ½, 6: target, small game, small game bird
- Shot size 5, 4, 2, BB: medium game, upland birds, turkey

STEEL SHOT
- Shot size 6: upland birds, small game
- Shot size 5, 4: upland birds, waterfowl, small game
- Shot size 3: small and medium waterfowl
- Shot size 2, 1, BB, BBB, T, F: medium and large waterfowl

Since there are no exact rules for selecting shotgun ammunition, this information is for general guidelines only. Consult ammo manufacturer's recommendations for more specific uses.

NOTES

TRACKING A WOUNDED DEER

AFTER THE SHOT
- Take note of the animal's reaction to your shot.
- Pay attention to which direction it ran, and note a reference point, like a tall tree or a large rock.
- Track with binoculars for as long as possible.
- Be very quiet, and listen for the animal crashing in the brush and leaves.
- Wait before pursuing and recovering.

COMMON REACTIONS TO HITS
- If the animal drops almost right away, it is probably a brain or spinal column shot.
- If the deer jumps slightly in the air, it is usually a heart or lung shot. Typically a deer will run about 200 yards with this type of hit.
- If the deer hunches up and its tail is down and runs away, it is usually a gut shot.
- A jump and stumble as it takes off running could be a shot to the legs.
- A liver shot is a kill shot with a lot of blood. Usually the deer will lie down within 200 yards and not get up again if left alone. Wait at least an hour before pursuing.

AFTER THE WAIT TIME TO LOOK FOR SIGNS
- Begin by marking the spot from which you took the shot.
- Look for blood, and mark the first place you find blood.
- Lots of hair might indicate a grazing shot.
- The darker the hair, the higher on the body the animal was shot. White hair indicates a gut or low shot.
- A small amount of hair may indicate a hit to the body.

- Bone fragments are usually signs of a hit to the leg.
- Look for blood chest-high.
- Blood signs about three feet off the ground can indicate a shot to the heart, lungs, or large blood vessels in that area.
- Blood with small air bubbles indicate a fatal shot. The deer should not be too far from the point of impact.
- Blood trails can disappear as bleeding slows and clotting begins.
- Try not to push a wounded animal.
- Blood mixed with green or brownish material indicates a gut shot and may also have a strong odor. Gut shots are the worst. Bleeding can almost stop as the animal runs and the blood is diverted away from the digestive system. Also, the intestines can actually plug the entrance and exit holes, limiting blood sign on the trail.
- Gut shot animals may require that you wait four to six hours before trying to recover.
- Look for tracks, kicked up leaves, and disturbed dirt, all of which are potential indicators of a deer's movement and direction.
- Wounded deer have a tendency to run downhill.

ADDITIONAL TIPS

- Blood trailing flashlights are available, which use colored lenses that help to illuminate the reflective properties of blood.
- Commercial powders are also available to sprinkle along the trail at night to illuminate a blood trail.
- If you jump a deer that has been hit, back off, and let it bed down again.
- As you follow a blood trail, walk to the side of the run so as not to disturb the trail in case you have to retrace your steps and pick up a lost trail.
- Don't forget to check the underside of leaves if you lose the trail.
- While tracking a wounded deer, if you jump a deer and it flags its tail, it is probably not your deer. Wounded deer rarely will "flag."
- Gut-shot deer tend to head for water. Check in the water for an expired deer.
- Use toilet paper to mark each sign or blood spot.
- Don't hesitate to get down on your hands and knees to look for signs.
- Look ahead of you while tracking. You may spot the deer from a distance and avoid jumping it again.

- Tracking in grass is difficult, as blood can fall all the way to the ground without staining the grass.
- Look for clusters of ants, flies, and daddy longlegs. These insects feed on blood.
- If you lose the trail, begin at the last marked sign, and walk in ever-increasing circles until you pick up the sign again.
- Listen for birds like jays and crows. They sometimes sound alerts where an animal lies dead.

NOTES

WHO WE ARE

EPHESIANS 1:11-19

11-12 It's in Christ that we find out who we are and what we are living for. Long before we first heard of Christ and got our hopes up, he had his eye on us, had designs on us for glorious living, part of the overall purpose he is working out in everything and everyone.

13-14 It's in Christ that you, once you heard the truth and believed it (this Message of your salvation), found yourselves home free — signed, sealed, and delivered by the Holy Spirit. This signet from God is the first installment on what's coming, a reminder that we'll get everything God has planned for us, a praising and glorious life.

15-19 That's why, when I heard of the solid trust you have in the Master Jesus and your outpouring of love to all the followers of Jesus, I couldn't stop thanking God for you — every time I prayed, I'd think of you and give thanks. But I do more than thank. I ask — ask the God of our Master, Jesus Christ, the God of glory — to make you intelligent and discerning in knowing him personally, your eyes focused and clear, so that you can see exactly what it is he is calling you to do, grasp the immensity of this glorious way of life he has for his followers, oh, the utter extravagance of his work in us who trust him — endless energy, boundless strength!

THINK

Consider your identity. Who are you — *really*? In what do you find your true identity and sense of worth? In other words, what makes you, you? Are the sources of your self-worth healthy or unhealthy? Jot down a few notes about how you see your identity.

READ

Read the passage silently, but mouth the words of the verses as you read. What does this passage say about your identity? What is Christ's role in shaping your identity? Refer to your notes. How does this picture of your identity compare to those initial thoughts?

PRAY

Paul includes several elements in his prayers for the church at Ephesus. It is full of thanksgiving, petitions for intimacy with the Father, clarity for direction, knowledge of a life lived with Christ, and strength.

Make Paul's prayer in verses 15-19 your own. For example, *I ask you — the God of my Master, Jesus Christ, the God of glory — to make me intelligent and discerning in knowing you personally.* And so on.

Next, ask God to bring to mind an individual who needs prayer. Come before God and pray these verses for that person's current situation and overall life. Pray for his or her identity. Make your prayer specific by replacing the applicable words in today's passage with the individual's name.

Are there others for whom you could pray this prayer? Spend time interceding for them as well.

LIVE

If the Spirit nudges you to do so, tell the person that you prayed specifically for him or her. Read that person the prayer from Scripture.

HOW TO SCORE A BUCK

(Boone and Crockett)

For official instructions for scoring your trophy you can refer to the score sheet available from Boone and Crockett Club at www.boone-crockett .org.

Scoring consists of the following measurements to the nearest one-eighth of an inch.

NUMBER OF POINTS ON EACH ANTLER
- To be counted a point, the projection must be at least one inch long, with the length exceeding width at one inch or more of length.
- All points are measured from tip of point to nearest edge of beam.
- Beam tip is counted as a point, but not as a measured point.

TIP-TO-TIP SPREAD
- The tip-to-tip spread is measured between the tips of the main beams.

GREATEST SPREAD
- The greatest spread is measured between perpendiculars at a right angle to the centerline of the skull at the widest point, whether across main beams or points.

INSIDE SPREAD OF MAIN BEAMS
- The inside spread of main beams is measured at a right angle to the centerline of the skull at the widest point between main beams.

TOTAL LENGTHS OF ALL ABNORMAL POINTS
- Abnormal points are those nontypical in location (such as points originating from a point or from the bottom or sides of the main beam) or extra points beyond the normal pattern of points.
- Measure in the same manner as typical points are measured.

LENGTH OF MAIN BEAM

- The length of the main beam is measured from the center of the lowest outside edge of the burr, over the outer side to the most distant point of the main beam.
- The beginning point is on the burr where the centerline along the outer side of the beam intersects the burr, then generally follows centerline to tip of point on the main beam.

LENGTH OF NORMAL POINTS

- Normal points project from the top of the main beam.
- They are measured from the nearest edge of the main beam over the outer curve to the tip.
- Lay the tape along the outer curve of the beam so that the top edge of the tape coincides with the top edge of the beam on both sides of the point to determine the baseline for point measurement.
- If there are more than five abnormal points to a side, add them together.

CIRCUMFERENCES

Circumferences are taken at the narrowest place:

- Between burr and first point
- Between first point and second points
- Between second point and third points
- Between third point and fourth points

NOTES

FIELD DRESSING YOUR DEER

Here are some simple steps to field dressing your deer, based on guidelines from the Ohio Division of Wildlife, Department of Natural Resources.

STEP 1
Display a hunter orange article high enough to be seen as a safety precaution. Next, organize the equipment you will need so that you do not have to reenter your pack with bloody or dirty hands. Take your time. Be safe.

STEP 2
Make sure the deer is truly dead. Approach from behind and, using a stick or similar object, touch next to the eye. If it twitches, then obviously the deer is not dead and may require a follow-up shot to humanely end any suffering and ensure your safety. Now, tag it according to state game laws.

STEP 3
Roll the deer onto its back. Carefully cut a small opening at the base of the breastbone (pelvis side). This cut should be only large enough to insert your fingers into the incision. Use your free hand to lift the skin, and continue cutting down the midline until you almost reach the navel. Avoid cutting into the stomach, as doing so may contaminate the meat. This incision should be at least twelve to fourteen inches long so the entrails can be extracted.

STEP 4
Roll the deer back on its side and pull out the stomach, liver, and intestines, being careful not to puncture or tear the stomach. Use your knife to separate the stomach and liver from their muscular attachments along the backbone. Once the entrails are removed, you will have access to the chest cavity.

STEP 5

Cut through the diaphragm that separates the chest cavity from the digestive organs. With both hands, reach in and hold the lungs out of the way with one hand. With the free hand and knife, reach as far forward as you can, and cut through the windpipe and esophagus. Remove the lungs and windpipe, cutting away any connective tissue. This will give you a clean chest cavity and a thorough bleed-out. Use extreme caution when reaching into the deer. There may be broken bones or even a buried broad head from an earlier archery shot.

STEP 6

You are almost done. To remove the rest of the digestive tract and bladder, it is a good idea to tie a string around the bladder and large intestine in order to prevent urine and fecal matter from contaminating the meat.

Cut around the anus from the outside of the deer. Next, insert your finger into the incision, lift the large intestine out of the way, and cut away any connecting tissue from the intestine and bladder. Gently pull the intestine from inside the body cavity, and remove the entire contents, including the anus that you cut free.

NOTE: Other techniques remove the bladder and intestine as a measure to reduce the chances of contamination. Gut shots will make this step more difficult. Be sure to remove as much contamination as possible and, if the meat is washed with water, be sure to thoroughly dry it with a rag or paper towels.

STEP 7

Try to cool the meat as quickly as possible, and transport it safely.

NOTES

HE IS SUPREME

COLOSSIANS 1:15-23

15-18 We look at this Son and see the God who cannot be seen. We look at this Son and see God's original purpose in everything created. For everything, absolutely everything, above and below, visible and invisible, rank after rank after rank of angels — *everything* got started in him and finds its purpose in him. He was there before any of it came into existence and holds it all together right up to this moment. And when it comes to the church, he organizes and holds it together, like a head does a body.

18-20 He was supreme in the beginning and — leading the resurrection parade — he is supreme in the end. From beginning to end he's there, towering far above everything, everyone. So spacious is he, so roomy, that everything of God finds its proper place in him without crowding. Not only that, but all the broken and dislocated pieces of the universe — people and things, animals and atoms — get properly fixed and fit together in vibrant harmonies, all because of his death, his blood that poured down from the cross.

21-23 You yourselves are a case study of what he does. At one time you all had your backs turned to God, thinking rebellious thoughts of him, giving him trouble every chance you got. But now, by giving himself completely at the Cross, actually *dying* for you, Christ brought you over to God's side and put your lives together, whole and holy in his presence. You don't walk away from a gift like that! You stay grounded and steady in that bond of trust, constantly tuned in to the Message, careful not to be distracted or diverted. There is no other Message — just this one. Every creature under heaven gets this same Message. I, Paul, am a messenger of this Message.

READ

Wherever you are, stand up and read the passage aloud. Stand prayerfully in a posture that communicates to God respect and receptivity to his Word.

THINK

This passage speaks of the supremacy and power of God manifested through Jesus Christ. What specific attribute or characteristic of Jesus sticks out to you most in this passage? Why do you think it does?

"We look at this Son and see the God who cannot be seen. We look at this Son and see God's original purpose in everything created." What are specific, practical ways in which you can "look at this Son"?

What does the following mean? "He was supreme in the beginning and — leading the resurrection parade — he is supreme in the end." What implications does this have in your life today? Wonder about the supremacy of Christ.

PRAY

Reflect on the attribute of Christ that struck you (for example, maybe it was that everything "finds its purpose in him"). In what ways would the world be different if Christ did not possess that attribute? In what ways would your life be different? How and why?

LIVE

Live your day knowing that you serve — and are loved by — the God who holds the entire world together!

SOLUNAR TABLES

These annual tables are used by fishermen and hunters to determine the best days of the month and the best time of the day for catching fish or hunting game.

Fishermen use tides, sunrise, and sunset to help determine when the fish might be biting. Hunters refer to the sun and moon cycles to help determine when the game might be moving.

In theory, the position of the moon in relation to an animal's body affects the animal's state of activity. Strongest activity times are believed to be when the moon is full or new. The weakest would be when the moon is one quarter and three quarters full.

PEAK DAYS
- The day of a new or full moon.
- Provides the strongest influence in each month.
- This effect can last for twenty-four hours and fifty minutes. (Approximate time between moonrises.)

PEAK MONTH
- June has more combined sun-moon influence than other months.
- During a full moon, the sun and moon are nearly opposite each other, with the shortest amount of time without one or the other being in the sky.
- During a new moon, the sun and moon are in near perfect rhythm, traveling the sky together with their forces combined.

PEAK TIMES
- When a solunar period falls within thirty minutes to one hour of sunrise or sunset
- When there is a moonrise or moonset during that period
- When the above times occur during a new or full moon

NOTE: Because of the interaction between the lunar and solar cycles, no two days, months, or years will be identical. Be sure to check current charts for up-to-date information.

PRAISE HIM, SUN AND MOON

PSALM 148:2-12

2-5   Praise him, all you his angels,
        praise him, all you his warriors,
    Praise him, sun and moon,
        praise him, you morning stars;
    Praise him, high heaven,
        praise him, heavenly rain clouds;
    Praise, oh let them praise the name of GOD —
        he spoke the word, and there they were!

6   He set them in place
        from all time to eternity;
    He gave his orders,
        and that's it!

7-12   Praise GOD from earth,
        you sea dragons, you fathomless ocean deeps;
    Fire and hail, snow and ice,
        hurricanes obeying his orders;
    Mountains and all hills,
        apple orchards and cedar forests;
    Wild beasts and herds of cattle,
        snakes, and birds in flight;
    Earth's kings and all races,
        leaders and important people,
    Robust men and women in their prime,
        and yes, graybeards and little children.

READ

Read the passage a few times aloud, zeroing in on each image. Allow the words to wash over you in their vividness: See specific birds or wild beasts, sense the chill of the ice, hear the roaring of the ocean. Watch every action of the characters. Compare the way each created thing uniquely praises its Maker.

THINK

In the silence that follows the reading, meditate on what you've seen and heard. With all these pieces of creation in the background, praising God, how do you see him? What is he like? Spend time thinking about him.

PRAY

Pick the character attribute of God that seems the most powerful after your meditation. Envision God in this role, then see yourself entering his presence. How do you respond to him? How does he treat you? Rest in God's presence or talk to him or adore him — whatever fits the scene.

LIVE

As you go through your day, pay special attention to natural objects around you (rocks, trees, animals, hills) as well as people (individuals, crowds). Observe how they glorify their Creator by their existence. Don't be overcritical or get caught up in evaluating — just notice.

HELPFUL KNOT KNOWLEDGE

The right knot can make the job easier or maybe even save your life. Not all knots are created equal. A knot is formed when a rope is tied to itself. A hitch is when rope is tied to another object. A bend is when a rope is tied to another rope. Choose the right knot for the right job.

Here are some common examples for each category on which to build your knot knowledge.

KNOTS
- Square knot
- Figure 8

HITCHES
- Clove hitch
- Two half hitches

BENDS
- Sheet bend
- Fisherman's knot (great for webbing)

NOTES

BEAUFORT WIND SCALE

In the early 1800s, Sir Francis Beaufort, an admiral in the British navy, developed a scale to communicate wind force. He based his scale on wave characteristics and the ship's sails. This scale is still used today as a common language for wind velocity.

The following chart includes sea use and an adapted scale for land use.

Beaufort Number	Wind Speed Knots (MPH)	Seaman's Term	Sea State	Effects on Land
0	Less than 1	Calm	Glass, flat, calm	Calm, smoke rises vertically
1	1 to 3 (1 to 3.5)	Light Air	Ripples, no foam crests	Smoke drifts with wind direction
2	4 to 6 (4.5 to 7)	Light Breeze	Small wavelets (6"- 8"); crests begin to break	Wind is felt on face; leaves rustle
3	7 to 10 (8 to 11.5)	Gentle Breeze	Large wavelets (2'); crests begin to break; scattered whitecaps	Leaves, small twigs, small flags move
4	11 to 16 (12. 5 to 18.5)	Moderate Breeze	Small waves (3') with numerous whitecaps	Dust, paper, leaves raised up; small branches move
5	17 to 21 (19.5 to 24)	Fresh Breeze	Moderate wave (6') and many whitecaps and some spray	Small trees in leaf sway; large flags ripple
6	22 to 27 (25 to 31)	Strong Breeze	Large waves (10') whitecaps everywhere with much spray	Larger branches of trees in motion; whistling can be heard in wires
7	28 to 33 (32 to 38)	Moderate Gale	Large waves (13'); foam blown in streaks; sea heaps up	Whole trees are in motion; resistance felt while walking against the wind

Beaufort Number	Wind Speed Knots (MPH)	Seaman's Term	Sea State	Effects on Land
8	34 to 40 (39 to 46)	Fresh Gale	Moderately high waves with longer length (18'); crests break into spindrift	Small branches and twigs are broken off; hard walking against wind
9	41 to 47 (47 to 54)	Strong Gale	High waves (23'); sea begins to roll; visibility is affected	Light structural damage occurs; roof shingle torn from roof
10	48 to 55 (55 to 63)	Whole Gale or Storm	Very high waves (30'); sea looks white as foam is blown in dense streaks; heavy sea roll; visibility is restricted	Moderate structural damage occurs; some trees uprooted
11	56 to 63 (64 to 72.5)	Violent Storm	Exceptionally high waves (35'); visibility is poor	Heavy widespread structural damage; large trees uprooted
12	Over 64 (over 74)	Hurricane	Waves may reach 45' in height; air is filled with foam and spray; visibility very poor	Very heavy structural damage; very large trees broken or uprooted

NOTES

_____

_____

_____

_____

_____

_____

_____

_____

_____

PERMITS AND LICENSES

Here are some useful sources concerning transporting firearms, carry permits, and hunting and fishing licenses.

INTERSTATE TRANSPORTATION OF FIREARMS

- Title 18, Part I, Chapter 44, § 926a

  Interstate Transportation of Firearms

  Release date: August 3, 2005

  Notwithstanding any other provision of any law or any rule or regulation of a State or any political subdivision thereof, any person who is not otherwise prohibited by this chapter from transporting, shipping, or receiving a firearm shall be entitled to transport a firearm for any lawful purpose from any place where he may lawfully possess and carry such firearm to any other place where he may lawfully possess and carry such firearm if, during such transportation the firearm is unloaded, and neither the firearm nor any ammunition being transported is readily accessible or is directly accessible from the passenger compartment of such transporting vehicle:

  Provided, That in the case of a vehicle without a compartment separate from the driver's compartment the firearm or ammunition shall be contained in a locked container other than the glove compartment or console.

- Complete information on Canadian firearms laws for residents and visitors, as well as fee lists and all required forms can be found on the Canadian Firearms Centre website at www.rcmp -grc.gc.ca/cfp-pcaf.

CARRY PERMITS

- For information in regard to states that will honor your carry permit, visit www.usacarry.com.

HUNTING AND FISHING LICENSE INFORMATION

- Beyond your backyard: If you are planning a hunting or fishing adventure but you are not familiar with the state license and permit regulations, here is a good place to begin your search: www.reserveamerica.com.

- This website contains links to each state's hunting and fishing regulatory agencies. Many offer online purchases of permits and even allow entering a state elk lottery.

NOTES

CREATION MOVIE

JOB 38:4-11,24-27

4-11
"Where were you when I created the earth?
  Tell me, since you know so much!
Who decided on its size? Certainly you'll know that!
  Who came up with the blueprints and measurements?
How was its foundation poured,
  and who set the cornerstone,
While the morning stars sang in chorus
  and all the angels shouted praise?
And who took charge of the ocean
  when it gushed forth like a baby from the womb?
That was me! I wrapped it in soft clouds,
  and tucked it in safely at night.
Then I made a playpen for it,
  a strong playpen so it couldn't run loose,
And said, 'Stay here, this is your place.
  Your wild tantrums are confined to this place.' . . .

24-27
"Can you find your way to where lightning is launched,
  or to the place from which the wind blows?
Who do you suppose carves canyons
  for the downpours of rain, and charts
    the route of thunderstorms
That bring water to unvisited fields,
  deserts no one ever lays eyes on,
Drenching the useless wastelands
  so they're carpeted with wildflowers and grass?"

READ

Read the passage aloud slowly.

THINK

Read the passage again aloud, noticing that this is a poetic account of the Creation of the world in contrast to Genesis 1, which is a narrative account. Think about the following questions, remembering to consider the "why" behind each one.

1. What is your favorite moment in this Creation story?
2. Are you more fascinated by God as a blueprints-and-measurements kind of being or as a tamer of ocean tantrums?
3. How do you respond to God as a lightning launcher or canyon carver?
4. For what part of God's creation would you have wanted a front-row seat (for example, a daisy, a zebra, or a waterfall)?

PRAY

Tell God your responses to these questions. What do you think might be God's response to you?

LIVE

Go for a walk or hike or run in a beautiful place. Notice every single detail of nature that you can, and take pleasure in thinking about how God created it.

THE FUTURE

Outdoor activities and adventures are for the moment, but they also must be preserved and managed for the next generation. Mossy Oak is a leader in conservation, tree management, and food plots.

HABITAT MANAGEMENT
- Managing wildlife begins with managing the habitat.
- Addition of natural elements, along with management, is at the heart of Mossy Oak's obsession with conservation.
- At Nativ Nurseries, their proprietary treatments focus on water, food, and cover elements of habitat building and restoration of habitat.
- They offer the healthiest stock and root systems available in their rapid mast system that results in faster plant growth and greater survival capabilities.
- Improving natural habitat is an obsession with Mossy Oak. When you are ready to provide your property and its wildlife the best that Mother Nature can provide, visit Mossy Oak Nativ Nurseries at www.nativnurseries.com to learn more about their efforts.

FOOD PLOTS
- Food plots play an important part in promoting healthy animals and bigger bucks.
- Utilizing food plots allows the land owner to supply the amount and quality of food necessary to promote this healthy growth that mere supplemental feeding cannot provide.
- They also decrease the average home range of each deer, thus increasing the property's carrying capacity.
- Deer are naturally browsers. Food plots offer a more natural environment for their feeding than standing at a feeder, with forage that is more palatable and digestible than corn, protein pellets, or native vegetation alone.
- Whitetail will consume no more than 25 percent of their diet from supplemental feed, but as much as 80 percent of their diet from food plots.

- To learn more about effective food plots, visit Mossy Oak BioLogic at www.plantbiologic.com.

Whether it is through Mossy Oak's brand camouflage, Nativ Nurseries, or BioLogic, Mossy Oak is dedicated to testing, questioning, and trying everything it does. It is a part of a relentless quest for perfection and for getting people closer to nature in more ways than one. "It's not a passion. It's an obsession."

NOTES

APPENDIX

THE BRIDGE TO LIFE

STEP 1 — GOD'S LOVE AND HIS PLAN

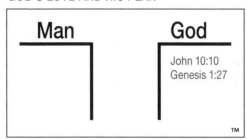

God created us in his own image to be his friend and to experience a full life assured of his love, abundant and eternal.

- Jesus said, "I have come that they may have life, and have it to the full." (John 10:10)
- We have peace with God through our Lord Jesus Christ. (Romans 5:1)

God planned for us to have peace and abundant life right now, so why are most people not having this experience?

STEP 2 — OUR PROBLEM: SEPARATION FROM GOD

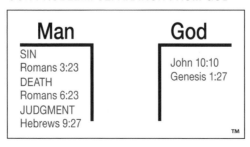

God created us in his own image to have abundant (meaningful) life. He did not make us robots to automatically love and obey him, but he gave us a will and freedom of choice. We chose to disobey God and go our own willful way. We still make this choice today. This results in separation from God.

- All have sinned and fall short of the glory of God. (Romans 3:23)
- Your iniquities have separated you from your God; your sins have hidden his face from you, so that he will not hear. (Isaiah 59:2)

On our own, there's no way we can attain the perfection needed to bridge the gap to God. Through the ages, individuals have tried many ways, without success. Good works won't do it (or religion or money or morality or philosophy).

- There is a way that appears to be right, but in the end it leads to death. (Proverbs 14:12)

STEP 3 — GOD'S REMEDY: THE CROSS

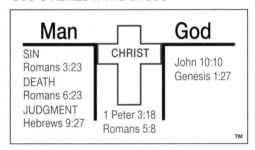

Jesus Christ is the only answer to this problem. He died on the cross and rose from the grave, paying the penalty for our sin and bridging the gap between God and people.

- Christ also suffered once for sins, the righteous for the unrighteous, to bring you to God. (1 Peter 3:18)
- There is one God and one mediator between God and mankind, the man Christ Jesus. (1 Timothy 2:5)
- God demonstrates his own love for us in this: While we were still sinners, Christ died for us. (Romans 5:8)

STEP 4 — OUR RESPONSE

Believing means trust and commitment: acknowledging our sinfulness, trusting Christ's forgiveness, and letting him control our lives. Eternal, abundant life is a gift for us to receive.

- God so loved the world that he gave his one and only Son, that whoever believes in him shall not perish but have eternal life. (John 3:16)
- Very truly I tell you, whoever hears my word and believes him who sent me has eternal life and will not be judged but has crossed over from death to life. (John 5:24)

Is there any reason why you should not cross over to God's side and be certain of eternal life?

HOW TO RECEIVE CHRIST

1. Admit your need (that you are a sinner).
2. Be willing to turn from your sins (repent).
3. Believe that Jesus Christ died on the cross to pay the penalty for your sins and rose from the grave.
4. Through prayer, invite Jesus Christ to come in and control your life through the Holy Spirit (receive him as Lord and Savior of your life).

WHAT TO PRAY

Dear Lord Jesus, I know I am a sinner and need your forgiveness. I know I deserve to be punished for my sins, and I believe that you died to pay that price and rose from the grave. I want to turn from my sins. I now invite you to come into my heart and life. I want to trust and follow you as the Lord and Savior of my life. Thank you for your forgiveness and the everlasting life I now have. Amen.

GOD'S ASSURANCE OF ETERNAL LIFE

If you've prayed this prayer and are trusting Christ, the Bible says you can be sure you have eternal life.

- Everyone who calls on the name of the Lord will be saved. (Romans 10:13)
- It is by grace you have been saved, through faith — and this is not from yourselves, it is the gift of God — not by works, so that no one can boast. (Ephesians 2:8-9)
- Whoever has the Son has life; whoever does not have the Son of God does not have life. I write these things to you who believe in the name of the Son of God so that you may know that you have eternal life. (1 John 5:12-13)

Receiving Christ, we are born into God's family through the supernatural work of the Holy Spirit who indwells every believer. This is called regeneration, or the "new birth."

WHAT NEXT?

This is just the beginning of a wonderful new life in Christ. To deepen this relationship, you should:

1. Maintain regular intake of the Bible to know Christ better.
2. Talk to God every day in prayer.
3. Tell others about your new faith in Christ.
4. Worship, live in community, and serve with other Christians in a church where Christ is preached.
5. As Christ's representative in a needy world, demonstrate your new life by your love and concern for others.*

---

* The Navigators, "The Bridge to Life," 2011, www.navigators.org/us/resources/illustrations/items/The%20Bridge%20to%20Life.

THE HAND ILLUSTRATION

The Hand Illustration shows us how to have a practical, working grasp on the Bible. It has been estimated that we remember:

- 5 percent of what we HEAR
- 15 percent of what we READ
- 35 percent of what we STUDY
- 100 percent of what we MEMORIZE

So a balanced intake of the Bible comes through hearing, reading, studying, and memorizing. Then as we meditate on Scripture during these four activities, the Bible content touches our lives in a more personal and specific way, helping us grow spiritually and become more like Christ.

Let us look in more detail at these five methods of learning from the Bible.

1. **Hearing** the Word of God from godly pastors and teachers provides us with insight from Bible study done by others. It also stimulates our own appetite for Scripture. (Taking notes can increase our ability to retain what we hear.)

   Consequently, faith comes from hearing the message, and the message is heard through the word about Christ. (Romans 10:17)

2. **Reading** the Bible gives us an overall picture of Scripture and is also the foundation of the daily quiet time.

> Blessed is the one who reads aloud the words of this prophecy, and blessed are those who hear it and take to heart what is written in it, because the time is near. (Revelation 1:3)

3. **Studying** the Bible is more in-depth than reading. It leads us to sound doctrine and personal convictions about the major teachings of Scripture.

> Now the Bereans were of more noble character than those in Thessalonica, for they received the message with great eagerness and examined the Scriptures every day to see if what Paul said was true. (Acts 17:11)

4. **Memorizing** God's Word prepares us to use the Sword of the Spirit to overcome temptation and provides verses at our fingertips for helping and encouraging others.

> How can a young person stay on the path of purity? By living according to your word. I seek you with all my heart; do not let me stray from your commands. I have hidden your word in my heart that I might not sin against you. (Psalm 119:9-11)

5. **Meditation** enhances the effectiveness of the other four methods of Scripture intake. Only as we meditate on God's Word (thinking of its meaning and application to our lives) will we discover its transforming power in our lives.

> Blessed is the one . . . whose delight is in the law of the LORD, and who meditates on his law day and night. That person is like a tree planted by streams of water, which yields its fruit in season and whose leaf does not wither. (Psalm 1:1-3)

ABOUT THE AUTHORS

J. R. Briggs serves as cultural cultivator of The Renew Community, and he is the founder of Kairos Partnerships. As part of his time with Kairos Partnerships, he serves on staff with The Ecclesia Network and Fresh Expressions U.S. J. R. and his wife, Megan, have two sons, Carter and Bennett, and live in Lansdale, Pennsylvania. He contributed to the devos in this trail guide.

Jan Johnson is a retreat leader and spiritual director and has written more than fifteen books, including *Invitation to the Jesus Life* (NavPress), *Enjoying the Presence of God* (NavPress), *Savoring God's Word* (NavPress), and *When the Soul Listens* (NavPress). She contributed to the devos in this trail guide.

Allen Owens is an avid outdoorsman and the director of OSY ministries in Mexico at ELEVÁRE International. He wrote the trail guide material.

Katie Peckham has an MA in spiritual formation and soul care from Talbot Seminary and works as a spiritual director in Orange County, California. She enjoys training for triathlons and traveling with her husband and daughter. She contributed to the devos in this trail guide.

Eugene H. Peterson is a pastor, scholar, writer, and poet. After teaching at a seminary and then giving nearly thirty years to church ministry in the Baltimore area, he created *The Message* — a vibrant translation of the Bible from the original Greek and Hebrew that is used in the devos in this trail guide. Eugene and his wife, Jan, live in his native Montana.